Alphabet Anecdotes

Maria Iskander

Alphabet Anecdotes

Copyright © Maria Iskander
First published 2025

ISBN: 978-1-7638032-4-4

All rights reserved. Without limiting the rights under copyright reserved above, no part of this publication may be reproduced, stored in or introduced into a database and retrieval system or transmitted in any form or by any means (electronic, mechanical, photocopying, recording or otherwise) without the prior written permission of the owner of the copyright.

I would like to acknowledge the Aboriginal and Torres Strait Islanders as the traditional custodians of the land.
I also extend my recognition to the Jagera and Meanjin Peoples, to whose lands I wrote this book on.
Finally, I pay my respects to the Jagera and Turrbal elders, past, present and emerging.

Published with the assistance of Angel Key Publications
https://angelkey.com.au

Immerse yourself into poetry that strikes a chord and expands your vocabulary.

Each season of poetry has its own characteristics, and different periods of life bring different experiences, challenges, and opportunities.

There are no good or bad seasons, but some seasons may feel more comfortable than others.

It is my hope that this book will direct your life intention to find meaning, truth, acceptance, and peace in all the seasons of life.

CONTENTS

Spring 1

Summer 61

Fall 97

Winter 151

A is for Agog

You are full of intense interest or excitement.
You make one eager to leave any type of confinement.
When I am captivated and enthralled by a thing or event,
I use you to characterize my anticipated intent.

I live to understand how to express you best.
From at school, work, family, or other major life events.
I am convinced that you are an enticing word to relay.
You make one enthusiastic by even the mundane.

You make me sometimes impatient to see, hear and do.
Ranging from the habitual things, to trying out something new.
I buckle myself and prepare for some new opportunities that come my way.
For when I do that, the anticipation comes to stay.

You are an addictive emotion that leaves me, an enthusiast, to wanting more.
You leave me with a sense of joy at my core.
From the sudden burst of sunlight through the clouds of a new year.
You make me enthusiastic, smiling ear to ear.

I suppose that is how it's going to always be.
You give me an air of excitement, eager anticipation, and glee.
And with the whole world turning into a green ball of envy and money languages,
You make me agog, to wait and see what this life has in store next.

B is for Bloom

You are a state or time of beauty
A sort of freshness and vigour.
You are a state or time of achievement.
A period of growth that suggests a 'before and after'.

You are a term used to describe a flourishing career innovation.
As well as a personal growth and positive transformation.
Possibly, in a more metaphorical sense, you are just as a flower blooms.
When a person finds their passion and life calling, they become you: bloom.

As you can manifest in various ways.
People see your presence in improved relationships, career advancements for days.
You signify meanings of a successful, fruitful and attractive life.
You, bloom, foster personal wellbeing, earthly honour, and quality time.

B is for Brave

You are the art of wielding mental and moral fortitude,
Tackling fear, danger, and life's curveballs head-on.
You are all about stepping into the unknown,
Daring to confront uncertainty, making a deliberate choice to grow.

Embracing whatever the future holds.
You can take on many forms.
From an adult standing firm in their beliefs, even when stakes are high,
To a child taking a leap of faith, granting forgiveness to every passerby.

Whether it's diving into the deep end or hitting the field in a new sport,
Embracing you, sparks inspiration, making things happen in its course.
I see you most vividly in my friend, Nebiat, but I call her Nebby for short.
Nebby is one who dares to step forward, a truly brave soul.

Even when shadows of fear, uncertainty, or peril loom large.
Nebby wears bravery like a badge, unflinching in the face of adversity and harm.
It's not merely the absence of fear that defines who she is,
Rather, it's her audacity to act despite it.

Embracing bravery can spark inspiration and create a ripple effect,
It reveals who your true allies are in this journey of life,
And most profoundly, open doors beyond the edge of comfort.

B is for Breathtaking

Something so stunning, thrilling, or astonishing,
Usually leaves you momentarily speechless and gushing.
I imagine gazing at a magnificent landscape from Australia to Egypt,
Both wonderful countries with richly diverse histories, Oh, what a captivating feeling!

Apart from travels I have taken, I have witnessed performances in theatre,
All of which captivated my soul —those moments sprung from creative ideas.
Indeed, I find myself overwhelmed with joy and wonder for this life,
And in each morning, I cherish moments that make me laugh or sigh.

Considering these reflections on the breathtaking nature of life:
I thank You for this incredible journey I've been given.
Even when I complain and join in venting,
This life You have given me, in all its Glory, is nothing short of breathtaking.

B is for Breezy

You could be a nod to the inspiring journey of Brianne "Breezy" Bochenek,
A remarkable young woman who has triumphed over adversity.
For at just 9 years of age, she faced an aggressive bone cancer,
Yet, emerged as a beacon of hope, sharing her story at TEDx LaJolla

Much like Brianne, you may simply evoke all delightful feelings,
A refreshment that encourages others to conquer their fair share of life's dealings.
You're the charming adjective that paints a day with a gentle yet invigorating breeze.
You are perfect for setting sail in this boat of life, and letting the winds' Order lead.

C is for Celestial

You are related to or suggested as being heavenly and divine.
You are connotated to heavenly beings, and visible heavenly skies.
With multiple meanings, you are related to spirit and divinities.
You are often used to describe things that bring a fragrance like Christianity.

Angels, stars, and planets are used to inhabit your outcome.
You can also refer to an inhabitant of heaven above.
You mean something or someone pertaining to an invisible or spiritual divine.
You, celestial, bring an ethereal bliss, supernal peace and comfort so sublime.

C is for Circadian

You are the rhythm to my temple's natural 24-hour clock.
You keep operating on a healthy wake-sleep cycle that never stops.
Affecting many other systems throughout,
From the physical, mental, to the behavioural inside and out.

You are the physical, mental, and behavioural changes that experiences,
Over a 24-hour cycle, , from dusk to dawn, and from light to darkness
Inevitably, you are the biggest influence on rhythms, stress, or food intake,
As well as physical activity, social environment, and temperatures that change.

I still believe that Christ created you to help one discern.
On what is right and wrong with this world.
I also still believe that Christ uses you to realign,
As well as sync the world to be compassionate and kind.

Determining when we sleep, you prepare us for changes that befall.
You regulate peak creativity and productivity in tasks- big or small.
You, circadian rhythm helps us to not standardize Divine and human interactions.
You, circadian rhythm, are the rhythm that determines our daily actions.

D is for Discombobulated

You sound like a kind of physical disease.
A slang word that makes one feel not at ease.
You also sound like a confused state.
A fancy word that makes one have a disoriented fate.

Where I don't know up from down, can't spell my name,
Or when I can't focus on a task, or remember my age,
It is then when I know you are there, bouncing in several directions at once.
You make me feel bothered and thrown out of balance.

After moving to a new country, America, I was taught contradictory things.
From working hard to find success, and not losing yourself for anything.
It was also easy to feel like I lost control.
It was easy to feel like I had nothing at all.

But I have learned from my friends in America,
How to push myself forward and get back on track.
Indeed, I like to sit down with a book or film, having a cup of tea.
Although it's something mundane and small, it brings me back to reality.

The merry go round of life is rooted in all our brains.
It is not specific for a certain food, work, or specific place.
So, whenever I let someone take the work out of my plans outside,
I find myself no longer discombobulated; but safe, supported and satisfied.

D is for Dreams

You are like a tapestry woven from our thoughts, images, desires, and emotions,
  Often reflecting our hopes for the future and the aspirations in motions.
You are not mere fleeting whims; rather, deep-seated ambitions,
  Cherished and valued, you are an intrinsic part of identity and essence.

These nocturnal narratives play a vital role in our lives,
  Aiding us in processing the emotions, memories, and experiences inside.
Encountered each day, you spark our creativity and problem-solving skills.
Some studies even hint how you contribute to our physical, mental and overall well-being.

Offering insights into our feelings, values, and beliefs.
You cultivate a sense of optimism and self-belief.
For many, dreams, make even a dull life worth living.
If only we'd let our dreams take flight, and watch them shape our journey!

E is for Enigma

Your origin traces back to the Greek "ainigma,"
Meaning "to speak in riddles", a challenge to our understanding: a phenomena.
A touch of your mystery can spark intrigue and keep others engaged,
Enhancing attraction and fostering a sense of excitement for all days.

You capture the essence of something that invites curiosity.
You are referred to something or someone shrouded in mystery.
When a person is labelled as you, they become a captivating puzzle that's pressing.
A sort of individual whose thoughts and intentions remain elusive, leaving others guessing.

Being called you, often carries a positive connotation.
Suggesting that one possesses an alluring depth and a unique reputation.
Distinguishing such people from the crowd,
Hints at a rich tapestry of traits that may seem contradictory around.

You are present if someone's motivations are puzzling at best,
Or if they embody a blend of characteristics that don't quite fit together again.
Similarly, grand concepts like quantum physics or the majestic Pyramids of Giza,
Can also be deemed you, an enigma that provokes wonder and contemplation.

E is for Epiphany

Derived from the ancient Greek term, you mean "manifestation"
It comes from an exhilarating moment,
When clarity strikes like lightning,
Illuminating your understanding in a flash.

You encapsulate those magical moments of clarity that can transform,
Our understanding of the world around us, and even ourselves.
While they often spring from new insights, they also rely on the wisdom,
Wisdom we've gathered along the way.

Imagine a sudden spark of insight that reshapes your entire outlook on life.
This could be a profound spiritual awakening, a groundbreaking time.
All these moments often arise from a whirlwind of experiences, recent and distant Signalling personal growth and reflection.

So, what makes you so special?
Here are some defining traits:
Sudden, you hit out of nowhere, leaving one in awe proximation.
Intuitive, you are a gut feeling that unveils a situation.

Enlightening, you shed light on a problem,
Rare, you offer a fresh viewpoint that doesn't come often.
When a radical shift occurs, it can be dubbed as you, an epiphany.
You're the transformative revelation, altering one's emotional experience and reality.

E is for Exquisite

You evoke a sense of extraordinary beauty, charm, or delight,
When I look at you, I awe at how particularly you are refined.
There are a few delightful ways to weave you into my own Era tour,
I can see you as an illustration of pure joy, somewhat captivating too.

Diving into a beloved book transforms my ordinary day into an exquisite escape,
Where every page feels like a luxurious indulgence and getaway.
Stepping away from the digital noise and immersing myself in the present day,
Unveils the exquisite beauty that life has to offer me, right here today.

E is for Exuberance

You are the vibrant burst of energy that fills my heart with joy and excitement.
It's that delightful spark that radiates from those who embody this spirited essence.
As I dive into the traits that define my lively soul,
I thrive in social settings, relishing the company of all.

My outlook on life is painted in bright, optimistic hues.
I guess you could say I have a knack for uplifting those around me,
Motivating friends to chase their dreams,
And family to have a zest for life, infectious, brimming at the seams.

Calling all fellow joy-seekers, in a circle of happiness in every place.
Be sure to foster this delightful habit as an exuberant individual,
Cultivating resilience, seeking happiness,
And cherishing all the good moments with grace.

F is for Friends

Who you spend time with, is usually who you become to be.
So, be sure to choose your friends carefully.
I choose to surround myself with people that have higher standards.
Since I was a kid, my mama warned me to wisely choose my friends.

Alas, I didn't listen, I thought to be Christian was to get along with everyone.
I had no margin; I just wanted to make many friends and have fun.
To everybody, I was a good person to listen and speak with,
I used my energy to make people feel win.

Sure, my efforts to bring joy to others was a great feat.
However, it didn't take too long before I was burned out within.
Fortunately, when I finished high school, I had new people to befriend.
These were people who talked about books, authors, and trends that were 'in'.

My friends at university were all for my betterment.
I slowly like a snail, came out of my shell to move again.
I am now the result of that exposure, where I started figuring out how the world works.
I learned how smart and innovative people affect lives for better and worse.

Similarly, at times, I was affected by bad influences in university as well.
But this made me realize how people bring you heaven or hell.
So, the people who did not help me become my best self,
Became no longer part of my life, as time would tell.

G is for Generous

Living a life of generosity is like painting the world with vibrant strokes of kindness. Where you share your time, resources, and attention with others.
With threads of love, solidarity, and unwavering commitment,
A life of generosity is a life brimming with kindness and goodwill.

Funnily enough, the magic of generosity doesn't just sprinkle joy on the receiver,
It also, albeit remarkably, enriches the giver.
As the Bible is a treasure trove of heartwarming tales that bring generosities,
It is clear as day, that individuals who selflessly gave, played a part in the prophecies.

This spirit of giving, with verses like Proverbs 22:9,
Reminding us how the generous will themselves be blessed for their tithe and time. for Truly blessed, we are, when we consider the downtrodden, lonely, and poor.
We become living proof on stories and verses of generosity once more.

G is for Graciously

You embody a spirit of kindness, helpfulness, and courtesy.
You can also evoke a sense of comfort, ease, or luxury.
When I think of you, I think of a delightful blend of charm
A good taste, wrapped up in the elegance of a generous heart.

Memories with you, paint a picture of politeness and benevolence.
I think of the birthdays, baptisms, New Year's, Easter and Christmas.
You always served as an exclamation, adding flair to surprise or emphasis.
You always navigated life's hurdles by anchoring yourself in it.

Mum, I miss you a lot that it hurts me deep.
This life is not the same, I wish you were with me.
I will always remember your consistent display of kindness- unrelentless,
A gracious aura that brought to all, an outward beauty, and inner elegance.

H is for Hope

In my little corner of this world, my heart has been formerly burdened:
For family members and friends facing challenges and heartaches.
From the unexpected medical diagnoses, financial struggles, betrayals
To the tragic and sudden deaths.

I have gotten to the point where I want to resort,
To the childish behaviour I once observed from afar,
Comprised of sticking fingers in your ears and singing,
"La la la la la … Go away! I can't hear you!" from the top of your lungs

Sometimes I just can't anymore with bad news.
I wish this emotional weight would break free from me.
Things I'm praying about, are never answered.
Confirming the repetition in my heart: life is hard.

Clearly, circumstances fray you: my hope, turning it into a fragile thing to hold on to.
The question then becomes: What am I hoping to see through?
Am I merely hoping for a good life for me, my family, and my friends?
Or am I hoping to see God's blessings during all of life's circumstances and plans?

Without a shadow of doubt or fear,
You, the hope I hold onto is not always crystal clear.
I may strive towards a positive outlook and way.
But I sometimes, feel like you are not here to stay.

Seeing the glass as half full, not half empty, doesn't mean I am always strong.
No matter what life throws at me, I find you to keep holding on.
My life will not always go my way, and I am starting to accept this reality.
For in finding a way to see the good, strengthens my Christianity.

My kind of hope keeps my brown eyes wide open.
It fills me with grace, integrity and honour.
The weight of whatever burdens my heart, then becomes small.
As I strive to live my best life, not devoid of resilience and hope.

You are a mechanism, developed by the human brain inclusive of mine.
You help me cope, with contexts and situations, unfavourable to survive.
With you, hope, I find my motivation to move forward and make intentions to strive.
In the worst of times, you drive me forward, keeping me alive.

I is for Integrity

You make me love being honest and having strong moral principles.
All because of you, I behave ethically and do the right thing, even behind closed doors.
When I have you, I always do the right thing and in all circumstances.
You give me courage to do the right thing, no matter the consequences.

Building a reputation of you, will take a long time,
After years and years on end, your essence in my life, will be defined.
Yet, despite it taking years to gain you, it takes seconds to lose you forever.
Hence, I vow to make sure this occurs, never.

I will never allow myself to do anything that would damage your place in my life.
Having you means that I am honest, ethical, and follow moral minds.
At work, I take your value seriously,
Recognizing my work friends and co-workers, while fulfilling my responsibilities.

With you, I recognize that humans make life well and good.
I promise to then, show gratitude, and make everyone feel understood.
From saying a simple "thank you" when someone helps me out.
I will also take the time to write a thoughtful note, albeit profound.

With you, I will go the extra mile to give their friend a gift,
Especially when they've supported me through a difficult time, or as French say, 'shit'.
As good humans, you and I all want to make other people happy, safe, and relaxed.
So, having you: integrity, isn't easy, but it fosters a resilient legacy made to last.

I is for Impeccable

You embody a state of perfection, unmarred by faults or blame.
Signifying a greater journey of living without sin or shame.
You make me own up to my choices, and embracing self-reception,
Encompassing virtues of integrity, dependability, and treating others with retrospection.

Mama , you taught me to speak with integrity, choosing my words wisely as food,
You helped me steer clear of white lies and half-truths.
Instead of allowing me to blend in the crowds of comfort and fame,
You pushed me to reflect authenticity, even if it makes others feel strange.

Be a beacon of honesty and kindness,
This mantra of yours stands out from the rest.
Mama, you have helped me learn how to treat others as they wish to be treated as best.

Goodness, you exuded goodness in everything and everyone.
You were the pillar or reliability for the entire family, and essentially anyone.
And that is why your presence should be a promise kept, and legacy framed,
For mama, you are impeccable, you will forever be my role model until we meet again.

I is for Incandescent

When heated, you glow with a brilliant light,
Radiating energy and charisma that stays the night.
With a lasting impression, you manifest in various forms,
Highlighting your vibrant nature that surpasses the norms.

In the realm of literature, "An Incandescent Life" by Logan Kieller comes to mind,
It was a book about a poetic journey,
A journey of self-discovery and growth in time.

Conversely, in the business world, incandescence can symbolize,
The spark of entrepreneurial spirit,
Showcasing how it innovation across various organizations, can unite.

Incandescence, you ultimately refer to the light emitted from heated materials,
Like a person who grows through life's hell and comes out glowing all neat.
Yet, we often overlook the brilliance of the present moment, no matter how painful,
Mistakenly believing that something better exists beyond our control.

I is for Integrity

You are like the guiding star that lead the Three Wise Men from the East,
Illuminating the path of ethical and moral living.
You embody the courage to stand by principles such as honesty,
Even when the going gets tough, you remind one take accountability.

Truth is my compass with you,
I speak openly and honour my commitments too.
Being consistent helps me keep harmony intact,
You motivate me to stay true to my promises.

With 'we listen but do not judge' sounds like a nice testament,
The truth of the matter is the world feeds off on judgement.
Judging people, we know or have not even met,
It can be hard to acknowledge a mistake or any misstep.

You are the grace to learn from mistakes and move forward, learn from them.
You cultivate trustworthiness, showing others that one can be counted on,
Time and again.

I choose you, integrity, to keep me in the straight and narrow,
You are a cherished quality and noble path,
Comprised of small acts that matter.

J is for Justice

At its very core, you mean "to make things right."
You are a relational term that demands a great price.
For the wrongs committed, you are there, so that right relationships can exist.
With you, I can be something more than my own fleeting feelings.

Revenge and justice tend to be blurred lines.
When someone thinks it is you, they want to take 'an eye for an eye'.
But you are not about getting back at someone who did you dirty.
You bring everlasting peace, whereas revenge leaves us feeling petty and empty.

You are about fairness, kindness, and equity.
You ensure that everyone is treated respectfully.
You, hold people, all people, accountable for their actions and words.
You also inspire all people into right relationships, and to move on forward.

Where revenge is motivated by anger, fear, internalised trauma and pain.
You, justice, are motivated by the gold heart of God, who remains the same.
You make our hearts yearn to make all things new and right.
You refresh and clean our souls to work hard, be kind, and live like Christ.

If we become motivated by you, instead of a moving target.
We would understand what it takes to bring real justice.
Real justice means to care for the foreigner, widow and orphan.
As well as defend the oppressed, show mercy, compassion, and live in Truth.

When all is said and done, nothing can be taken back, unless we openly confess.
Particularly how you serve to support others, and people we have not yet met.
So, I hope I can do more, to support marginalised communities.
And ensure people, all people, through acts of justice, to feel included in society.

Through you, I can embody goodness in my core being.
Through you, I can break the barriers that prevent people from dignified living.
Justice, you give me courage and urgency, to stand up against,
All the discrimination and violence that destroys the humanity's common sense.

By applying you, daily as I brush my teeth.
I can contribute to making a difference, a real one.
From the bottom to the top,
Accessing freedom, dignity, and joy for everyone.

K is for Kindness

You are a quality we have been ignoring for too long.
You are the quality of being gentle, caring, and not recounting a wrong.
It always feels good to be treated with you, from someone.
And it's easy to be kind with all the people we love.

But how do we be kind, truly kind, to people who we hate?
You know the people I am talking about, it's the people who secretly disdain.
The kind of people who we may not know on a personal level.
People like rude drivers, passer byers, and people who think they know it all.

To be intentionally kind to people who do not like us or show respect.
We may justify that you, kindness, does not apply to 'them'.
So, the 'us' vs 'them' narrative comes up to stir the pot.
Making you, an exclusive act, which you are not.

So, how to deal with rude people who get under our skin?
Well, maybe we can consider making their presence not fall within.
Taking back our power, and blood pressure, we can learn quickly by time.
How people are just people, like us, there's no need to complicate it, let's be kind.

Being kind does not mean we become like a rug for people to step on willy nilly.
Being kind means you are true to yourself, whilst showing kindness intentionally.
So, when I show hesitation to have you, kindness to those who hurt me.
I will push myself to go the extra mile, with wisdom and a nod to my Christianity.

Showing you off, a little kindness, works like a snowball effect.
For kindness begets more kindness, each time I use it in suspect.
Indeed, one of the most important things I can ever do,
Is to be like bee, taking in beauty, and seeing the good in people too.

And where there is cynicism, cruelty, and meanness in the cyberspace online.
I can see the patterns and be like a goldfish going against the tide.
Afte going against the social norms and expectations to fight fire with fire,
I can transform the standard of you, making it intrinsically wired.

All of us, at the end of the day, are unkind at times.
So, if we expect God to be kind, overlooking our ingratitude at times.
We must also do the same for people in our lives.

You should be our personal intention, whether reciprocated or not.
If we each make an intention to be kind, then you, kindness, will blossom from all of us.

K is for Kinaesthetic

Springing from the word "kinesthesia," which means body's ability to sense movement. You are a phenomenon, a fascinating one, that occurs when our brain receives signals. Signals from our muscles and ligaments, letting us know how we're moving.
I think of dancing, although I can't dance, but it is an expression that will do!

A kinaesthetic learner thrives on real-world experiences and physical engagement.
They grasp concepts best through action, touch, and manipulation.
These learners love to act out scenarios,
Which deepens their understanding and helps them connect the dots to real-life.

For kinesthetic learners, hands-on experiences are the key,
The key to unlocking knowledge to see.
These learners prefer to stay active while learning,
Making games and physical activities invaluable tools for cementing concepts.

Everyday examples of kinaesthetic learning abound:
From cooking and baking, to gardening or riding a bike in town.
I hope as a teacher, I can nurture the kinaesthetic learning in practise, no pressure,
Thereby enhancing my student's social skills, while making learning an adventure!

L is for Love

You are a core aspect of God's Character.
Indeed, you are an attribute of God that makes us, fallen humans, better.
'God is love', I have heard this Bible verse, as a cherished sort of sentiment.
God being love, proves that you are in the purest form, create no inner conflict.

It is admirable that you are a word synonymous with God.
For when we use you, we remember our familiar and sacred bonds.
From saying: "I love this song, I love this show, I love this pet, or I love you".
You are the most profound words, made of six letters, and that breaks through.

You are one of the most time-consuming emotions in this life.
A combination of attraction and closeness, you make even the dullest people shine.
People we're very close to, is usually, if not always, is the one we share love with.
Such a person can be a friend, parent, sibling, or even our pet, we take in.

You are more than a fleeting feeling, attraction or affection.
When we feel you for someone, truly, we put them first, above even our own needs.
We care about them, their feelings
And work to maintain their overall wellbeing.

We may go out of our way to ensure the people we love are okay.
Gold hearts filled with you, love, leads to compromise and sacrifice our way.
Replacing our comforts to satisfy what another needs.
You are the action that makes us, a formerly blind shell, able to see.

While sight is the case of loving people each day,
There are eight different types of love that make us brave.
All types of love, according to Greek mythology and ancient times,
Serve a certain purpose and quality in our lives.

The first type of you, is called Familia, referring to family connections,
You are a kind of love that involves siblings, cousins, and parents.
Interestingly, the second love is classified as the Eros kind.
You are what we feel with a partner, broadly understood as 'romanticised'.

Here comes the third kind of love, based on a Christian principle – Agape
You are not based on emotions but on principles.
You are the love for people we do not like, a love that extends to the unlovable.

Welcome the fourth love called Philia.
Based on the Greek roots, you mean brotherly, and entail
A love whom we hold as dear as family, people not familial by blood.

L is for Luminous

Time after time,
You have read the story or seen a film,
When one finds themselves in a state of altered consciousness,
Encountering the Light that can feel like a direct brush with the divine Him.

This experience raises intriguing questions about the nature of scientific proof.
It makes us delve into the world of light that dazzles in the brilliance!
I think of the radiant sun and the flickering flame of a candle,
As well as the moon and our very own Earth, basking in the sun's glow.

You are often associated with positivity,
Evoking images of radiant faces, captivating performances in any vicinity.
Does anyone remember Owl City's Fireflies?
And how these magical creatures were described?

The fireflies were described as lighting up the night,
A mesmerizing chemical reaction known as bioluminescence.
Apart from Fireflies, other animals make the luminous light,
From Glowworms to Anglerfish that use luminous bacteria to survive.

In contrast, non-luminous objects are those humble items that don't shine on their own.

Think of everyday objects like chairs, tables, and cornerstones.

Overall, the concept of luminosity extends beyond mere objects, animals or science,

Luminous light can also unlock our human health, happiness and purpose for life.

M is for Magic

Life is brimming with magic.
This saying captures the essence of existence, defying logical explanation.
With wonder and intrigue abound,
Beauty in the ordinary and the extraordinary transforming our world into enchantment.

Embracing a magical life means taking the reins of your whole being
Acknowledging that you are the architect of your reality—both consciously and subconsciously.
You possess the power to reshape your brand of magic and triumph with tenacity.
While we may not achieve greatness, we can overcome our battles with bravery.
Crafting your own magic isn't merely about daydreaming.
It's about taking deliberate, consistent steps, acting like you mean it.

Start small, and don't be disheartened by setbacks that occur.
True magic unfolds when you invest effort, glean wisdom, and keep pushing ahead. Each tiny step you take is a vital piece of the grand mosaic.
Magical thinking is the whimsical belief that your thoughts or actions can create.

Creating tangible outcomes, even when there's no clear logical link, sanity.
Magic often manifests in the idea that certain actions—like knocking on wood—
Can ward off calamity.

A magical life is one that sparkles with joy, delight, and gratitude boundless.
It's all about letting go of grudges, being kind, and expending your world view.
So, go forth and embrace the magic that life has to offer!
Be yourself, start a healthy habit, and connect with one another.

N is for Nurture

She is all about caring for, feeding, and safeguarding someone or something.
Such as the little children, or tender plants, that grow from nothing.
She dreams of staying home to nurture her children,
Pouring love into their development, giving all her attention.

She represents the myriad external influences that shape anyone coming into this world.
As the rich soil that nourishes a seed, measures how much of who we are, crafted,
Crafted by nature versus nurture,
These are psychological traits, not just any words.

She encompasses all the environmental elements that shape human development, Including the way we are raised, our socioeconomic backdrop, formative childhood.
Whether it's fuelling your body with nutritious meals, ensuring restful slumber.
Or sticking to regular exercise routine, experiences, and habits that steal the thunder.

She is the epitome of experiences, education, and the habits we cultivate everyday.
She can be the key to unlocking a harmonious and uplifting lifestyle we portray.
Nurture, you capture the essence of the external factors that shape our self-esteem,
You are a woman of impact, baptizing us in confidence and empathy.

O is for Opportunities

O, you're the fifteenth letter of the English alphabet.
You're also one of the most positive letters that have a nice sound to it.
O, you are the Chemical symbol for Oxygen,
Making you the letter for the most important life element.

Now, the word that I find most appealing is opportunities.
According to the dictionary, opportunity means "time to possibly do something".
So, as this word means a world of possibilities,
I can be someone to find an opportunity in every situation or occasion.

Everyone wants to be a very happy or successful person.
It is not easy, and it takes a lot of deliberate effort to do so.
Most of us wait for an opportunity to come up,
And when all the variables are favourable to us.

But how often does that happen in real life?
Not everything is ever 'perfectly' aligned.
I want to find you, where it is not obvious.
I want to see the opportunity in every difficulty I face.

Let's be the people who can spot an opportunity in every situation.
In every recession, every pandemic, every war, and every devastation.
Let's seek you, an opportunity, for exploration, not exploitation.

Every situation that appears negative has a positive side to it as well.
I want to find you, an opportunity, for progress, and for doing good work.
I even think I will find opportunity in philanthropy,
Then for creating something new and starting a fresh journey.

You are perhaps the most important quadrant of a SWOT analysis.
While negative situations are opportunities for some,
It takes a lot more effort to be viewed positively, united.
A positive situation or technological advancement has obvious opportunities.
During the Covid-19 pandemic, this was apparent by many means.

You come in a life changing turning point in time,
You serve to revive our environment, create more familial and social life.
You invite us to learn new skills and build new behaviours.
Even the emotions of fear and danger become a life changer.

When all is said and done, the successful people in our life,
Seized an opportunity, often than not.
The successful people looked for ideas and trends,
All of which they bent and twisted into uniquely theirs.

Even though it requires a great deal of personal grit to look for you: opportunities,
It is good to work on our minds, like an elite athlete going to train.
For when we can train our minds to do this with might.
We can have you, opportunities, while striving to do what is right.

P is for Perspective

You are the lens through which we view the world around us.
A unique filter that colours our experiences and keeps us grounded.
Shaping our responses to life's happenings and opportunities, at times surprising.
You help us embrace a fresh perspective, a zeal to keep rising.

You can be a powerful tool for acceptance and happiness.
Allowing us to see opportunities where we once saw obstacles in our heads.
And the more we open ourselves to new chances and viewpoints,
You have shown us a richer and more satisfying life that one can't pinpoint.

I think of you as a personal way of interpreting the world.
If you believe that toys are detrimental to children's wellbeing,
Then a toy store might seem like a sinister thing.

Or if you think of relationships being rigid, set to societal norms,
You may struggle with keeping any relationship, which then leaves you torn.
Our perception is the compass that guides our lives,
Influencing how we view the world, interact with others, and use our time.

While this may be the case, it is essential to remember,
How no two perspectives are identical.
Each person's viewpoint is unique from individual experiences.
By shifting our perspective, we can find greater joy and acceptance.

Perspective, you are a fascinating concept.
Unlike a camera that captures a single view,
Even our brains then merge these perspectives to help us understand,
How there are many angles that make a woman or man.

Every individual has a distinct way of seeing the world.
Even when we share a language, misunderstandings can arise because we can't always concur.
Each other's thoughts and feelings, this is crucial to recognise,
At the same token, we may never fully grasp another person's experience,
No matter how hard we tried.

P is for Pedagogy

With roots tracing back to the Greek words "paidos," meaning child
And "agogos," meaning leader
Pedagogy dances around the realm of education as needed.

Embodying the art and science of teaching.
It encompasses both the teaching profession,
And is often explored in a higher education setting.

At its core, pedagogy is the act of imparting knowledge.
An approach where the teacher takes in their pedagogical journey.
With the teacher taking the lead, there is influence,
Influence on the students' actions, strategies and decisions.

A multifaceted concept extending beyond traditional classrooms,
Is the crux of pedagogy, as it always finds a way in knowledge acquisition.
Pedagogy, you are woven from various teaching methods and learning tasks,
You shape students with a multitude of matters and influences that last.

P is for Philanthropic

Simply to love humanity is to blossom in the spirit of giving.
Giving time, food, treasure or talent.
Today, it is important to uplift the lives of others.
I imagine the joy of making a monetary contribution,
To a cause that resonates with your heart!

For some, philanthropy manifests as substantial financial donations,
All of which help fund groundbreaking research, scholarships or a building.
At its core, philanthropy is about enhancing the human experience and impact.
It's a powerfully noble calling, regardless of anyone's financial standing intact.

Philanthropy, you are a beautiful expression of altruism,
Dedicated to the greater good and the enhancement of quality of life.
You stand to provide public acts of love for humanity,
Making this broken world more kind.

Q is for Quirky

You are a delightful friend that captures the essence of the wonderfully weird.
Dancing to the beat of your own drum, you flaunt an eccentric charm, hard to ignore. Whether it's a peculiar trait, an unpredictable behaviour, or an offbeat appearance,
You are all about those delightful norm deviations.

Celebrating you—charmingly odd and standing out in a crowd.
You have a sense of humour that can make even a grinch laugh.
Scratching my head in amusement about your refreshing authenticity,
You are as rare as a unicorn, a friend with a knack to always surprises me, quirky.

R is for Rare

Rare in the finest definition means seldom occurring or found uncommon.
It is marked by an unusual quality, appeal or distinctive merit.
He calls me rare because I mean the world to Him.
He calls me rare because I am His everything.

I am rare because I have exceptional qualities that He finds attractive.
He values my personality, intelligence, values, interests combined.
I am rare because of the factors that make me stand out from the world.
He makes me feel like I am "one-of-a-kind" and not easily replaceable.

I am recognized as set apart on my individuality,
He makes me feel seen and heard, connecting me on a deeper level.
I am defined with my behaviours that match my intentions clearly.
My "rarity" suggests I find every chance I can, to support people.

Everyone will be wowed by all my consistency.
I love to carry out my morals, values and integrity.
He calls me modest by embracing both strengths and weaknesses.
When I am complimented, I smile and thank others for working just as hard as me.

Being rare is about strength and resilience:
I try my best to present my best self as it is.
Doing so, definitely takes a lot of work."
Being humble about being a 'rarity' is my area of growth.

R is for Rejuvenate

You are all about transcending mere self-care,
To weaving together the myriad benefits life has to offer.
Embracing you with consistency and flair,
At its core, will transform anyone, anywhere.

You are the art of breathing new life into the old,
Transforming the weary into bold,
You are about revitalizing what has lost its spark,
Infusing it with fresh energy and enthusiasm that lasts.

Think of it as a delightful revival, a refreshing makeover for your spirit and surrounds.
Embarking on new habits—like diving into meditation or being sound.
To rejuvenate your life is to rekindle that youthful zest, vigour, and spice
So be sure to sprinkle a little rejuvenation into your spirit and life.

R is for Resilient

You are like a sturdy tree that bends but doesn't break in the storm.
An ability to navigate through life's rough patches while still feeling strong.
Despite containing the full spectrum of emotions—anger, sorrow, and pain
You are the light that helps one to keep moving forward, both in body and mind again.

You are not merely about enduring hardships or going it alone.
It's the clearer lens through which to view our challenges, that help us overcome.
With a solid foundation of emotional resilience, we can face adversity with grace,
And poise, safeguarding our mental well-being along the way.

S is for Spellbinding

You capture the essence of something so utterly captivating,
A special something that ensnares my attention as if by magic.
It's the kind of fascination that leaves me spellbound, completely absorbed,
When something is described as spellbinding, it's not just my trail of thought.

It's a thrilling experience that enchants and mesmerizes.
I think of previous performances that left me breathless,
Or images and sounds that linger in my mind.

So, whether it's a performance that earns accolades, a documentary that captivates,
Or individuals in your life, like in mine, who pulls at your heartstrings every day,
The spellbinding nature of these experiences and moments.
Makes them unforgettable on purpose.

S is for Spontaneity

Imagine breaking free from the chains of procrastination.
Imagine rediscovering the joy and humour of your youthful generation.
Living spontaneously means trading the comfort of predictabilities,
For the thrill of the unknown, making life a delightful adventure filled with possibilities.

Spontaneity is like dancing to the rhythm of your own heart,
Where you let your impulses lead the way and make choices based on your heart.
Spontaneity is a vibrant way of living in the moment,
Rather than getting bogged down by endless planning.

To be spontaneous is to shake off the prison cell of overthinking,
And embrace the freedom to respond to life with a fresh perspective, winning.
It's about making quick decisions based on your current emotions and stories,
Allowing you to be fully present, savouring each experience with no little to no worries.

T is for Trust

You are the core belief that someone or something can be counted on.
From people doing what they say they will, to events occurring when advertised.
You are the key to the door of social relationships,
You are the foundation for peace, serenity, and cooperation.

You are critical for all romantic relationships, friendships, and families.
You flavour the interactions between strangers, and diverse social groups.
Whereas a lack of trust in such scenarios can come with serious difficulties.
For instance, a society on a whole, would likely fail to function properly.

Trusting unknown people may seem ill-advised,
However, having you is something people do every day, without even realized.
Trust, you are the element of letting go of things or people we cannot control.
You make us strong yet vulnerable.

U is for Understanding

A heartbeat of deep connections.
The cozy blanket that wraps us in emotional safety.
When we feel truly seen and empathically grasped,
Trust blossoms, and intimacy flourishes all around.

It's a sense of being understood that is crucial for us to navigate,
Our logical, emotional, and spiritual landscapes.
Fostering a sense of security and trust in our relationships,
Can help us decode our own place in this universe and recognise others' emotions.

The long debate over whether feeling loved or understood holds more weight,
Is a mere distraction from how to find respect and issue a validate.
Life is a vibrant mosaic of individuals, each a unique blend of cells that strengthen bonds.
We all are capable of growth, connection, and paved transformation.

As research by Dr. Stephen R. Covey highlighted over the recent years,
A life with understanding, is a life far richer and fulfilling.
To enhance our understanding, we can practice now,
Thereby offering a treasure trove that is all-round.

V is for Vicarious

You are a delightful term that captures the essence of living,
Living through the experiences of others.
Almost like wearing their shoes for a day.
It's that magical feeling of tasting life's adventures in a different way.

Through the stories and escapades of those around you.
You can imagine yourself on stage dazzling.,
Or you can imagine how you're basking in the glow of stardom.
A type of living through another's phenomenon.

Some folks channel their unfulfilled dreams into their children.
Sometimes these folks thrill by watching someone else take the plunge.
Even scrolling through the highlight reels of others' lives can bring a rush,
A rush of vicarious pleasure, as you sit in your room, cheering them on.

From time to time, you might consider these scenarios that occur in your life:
From absorbing wisdom from the tales spun in movies, books, or podcasts.
To dreaming through others, living out your aspirations instead of forging your own path.

But here's a gentle nudge: if you find yourself living vicariously too often,
Then it might be time to step out and embrace your own adventures.
After all, while it's fun to share in the escapades of others and their memories,
Nothing beats the thrill of picking up new habits and crafting your own stories!

W is for Worthy

Worthy is usually a verb link adjective for a person or thing.
To describe a person or thing as worthy, is to say it means something.
You are worthy because you are called and have the qualities or abilities required.
You are more than just enough; you are valuable, and one of a kind.

Worthy, that is who you are.
Truly deserving of unadulterated love.
So, the sooner you come to believe that you are worthy, my dear one.
The better off in this life, will you become.

Usually, to believe you are worthy, is far easier said than done.
I, myself, had trouble accepting my own worth for so many years to come.
I used to think that if I was not chosen for marriage particularly,
That I was not worthy to anyone clearly.

You too, perhaps have experienced a strange conundrum of thought.
A thought where people or social media expectations, make you feel distraught.
I have also had many people in my life who have told me and made me feel like I was never enough.
Yet, after setting strong boundaries, I resumed to feel worthy and loved.

Worthy are you, the person reading this poem today.
Regardless of your past experiences, you must come to a better place.
A place where you truly, deeply believe of your worthiness.
Manifesting respect, praise, and surpassing peace.

Even when many wolfish voices scream nonsense to control our minds,
We can listen to the gentle whisper, which confirms our innate worth from the beginning of HIS time.

X is for Xenophile

X, you are the most difficult letter of the alphabet.
A word that starts with X, Xenophile, has Greek roots meaning "stranger to men".
A true xenophile has deep, warm feelings for people across the globe.
A xenophile, has a fascination with cultures, known and unknown.

For some, to be a xenophile means to have a general preference for foreign faces.
Others could say, it is a state of being, attracting anyone to foreign cultures and places.
Such would be a positive syndrome to have when you are a world traveller.
Indeed, to be a xenophile is far better than to be a xenophobe for the matter.

Xenophobes are the people afraid of the unknown.
Irrationally, xenophobes dislike and fear people outside of their comfort zone.
If you are a xenophobe, then you should stay home.
But if you're a xenophile, keep celebrating every culture, as if it is your own.

Y is for Youth

Youth, you are defined as the period between childhood and adult age.
When God created man to live in this world forever,
He intended we use our complete energy as a youth.

So, I do not believe that it was in the divine plan for man to grow old and die.
We can say that God honours the youthfulness as a living sacrifice.
Like David the Psalmist offered a sacrifice of thanksgiving to God, sweet as honeydew,
David confirmed that our youth is like eagles' wings, daily renewed.

As Pope Shenouda III would say and pray:
Youth are the future of the church today.
Without youth, we cannot manage the world circumstances, good and bad.
In St Paul's words, the hope of youth, makes God glad.

Youth, it is defined as St. Paul advised his disciple, the young bishop's. Timothy.
To be a youth is to show respect for all men, their thoughts and different personalities.
Youth, you are our hope to be successful in all aspects of this 'blip' we generously call life.
Youth, you are our ability to be strong and have the word of God abide.

Youth, you call us all to challenge the wicked world,
A world filled with sin, Satan, and death, allusions to a Hellish underworld.
Nothing and no one can overcome these terrible things and situations.
Like Solomon, the wise and experienced man asked for,
Youth must be cheerful as a sign of their victory, for all nations.

Through the spirit of victory, youth can prepare themselves for Heaven.
Living a life with bravery and joy, while following the commandments.
Youth, you remind us of how God the Creator, draws near to all.
Even before the difficult days come, our youth carries us when we fall.

Without a doubt, the role of all members of the Church, especially the youth,
Shall come to pass afterward to pour out God's spirit, making a breakthrough.
Before you know it, all your sons and daughters shall prophesy to your youth,
While your old men shall dream dreams and your young men see visions too.

Z is for Zeal

You are the noun to confirm great enthusiasm and energy.
In pursuit of a cause or an objective, you give assurance to endure anything.
From bearing a misfortune, to the joy of partaking in various activities,
You wrap our bodies with brave bliss in uncertainties.

During all the blissful and positive times in our lives,
May we, at least for the most part, approach our days with natural excitement inside.
By all accounts, you are an infectious character trait to carry.
You make one to find the will to push ahead, in all reasons besides monetary.

You are the ardent and eager interest in pursuing something, usually great.
Beyond the curiosities that murder the cats, a zeal's beyond submitting to one's fate.
You provide a warmth feeling that makes one shine and glow.
You make one passionate to live like a flower, look pretty and grow.

Alas, for me, my journey to live with you, zeal, started at a dark time,
A time when I recovered from a decade-long illness of mine.
This illness had consumed me for so very long,
So, I didn't know how to live without it, I didn't feel like I belonged.

Thankfully, my miraculous healing and recovery showed me this truth,
That I wasn't truly living, so I decided to 'get busy living' as one should.
By 'getting busy living', I re-learned how to have zeal for things that mattered:
From God, my friends and family, I embarked on a figurative and literal journey.

After growing in my relationship with God, seeing Him as a Heavenly Father and friend,
I developed deeper friendships in my nuclear and extended family again.
I then figured out what I enjoyed doing in my spare time,
This included writing, which I learned to finally prioritize.

Now, it's not enough that I'm living my life with zeal,
I want you to do it, too!
It is my hope that with zeal, you will live out the grace and hope,
That only God can nurture in you, and ultimately reveal.

A is for Alchemy

In the grand scheme of life, you are the process of transforming oneself.
Through experiences, you shape character, resilience, and growth.
You also deepen one's relationship with the sacred dimension of life.
You, being a transformation through creation, work wonders day and night.

With you, life becomes recognised as the journey filled with ups and downs.
Joys and sorrows, victories and defeats, you call this a process that resounds.
By moulding us into who we are and are meant to become.
You ensure we understand and embrace the inevitable struggles that inevitably come.

Clearly, you are be applied to the book of life.
You help one to accept struggles and take pain on the stride.
You inspire us to be transformative from the struggles too.
Shifting our mindset to what we can, not cannot do.

A is for Anthropomorphise

You are the practice of attributing human characteristics, emotions, or behaviours,

To any non-human entities including objects, animals, and supernatural phenomena.

You're famously known as SpongeBob SquarePants and Winnie the Pooh,

As well as Thomas the Train Engine, and Simba from the Lion King 1 and 2.

You are the tendency to attribute human forms so fundamental.

You are a relevant comparison that's beneficial, and sometimes determinantal

Consciously or unconsciously, you occur in a way for people to interact,

With themselves, and others in the world, as a matter of fact.

Pet owners, we love them, or love to hate them, paradox of sorts.

Pet owners, you are usually the culprits that anthropomorphize, no afterthoughts.

Yet, even for those who don't own pets of any kind,

Can find themselves placing personality characteristics, a talent to anthropomorphize.

B is for Beloved

Capture the essence of something or someone that holds a special place in your heart. It can refer to a cherished individual, a pet, or even a treasured item that brings you joy. You may even refer to a favourite novel, a trusty bicycle, or a meaningful keepsake,
As a beloved item that makes your heart and mind elevate.

Saint John the Apostle, was affectionately dubbed the "beloved disciple,"
He not just a follower of Jesus; he was a cherished companion all in, for life.'

As one of the original Twelve Apostles, St John also had ultimate honours,
From sitting beside Jesus during the Last Supper, standing at the foot of the cross,
To supporting and looking after Jesus' mother at his home.

Sharing in those sacred moments of people we love, we can be like St John,
A presence during the harrowing of times.
We can also provide a unique perspective,
Capturing the essence of several monumental events.

Speaking of monumental events, we can also serve as a guiding light,
For spiritual and non-spiritual people, we meet in broad sight,
Thereby contributing heartfelt epistles, in the way we live our life.

C is for Charisma

You are a personal quality that can be developed and improved over time.
You have special traits that attract, fascinate and inspire.
You are often manifested in a confident and assertive aura that pleases many.
You embody excellent communication skills, human warmth and deep empathy.

You can also be engaging, and make others feel valued in sight.
As a moth goes to a flame, people gravitate to your light.
You're a quality that charms and can reek influence from a mile.
Giving people undivided attention, you are fully present with a smile.

Alas, some people abuse your superpower and gift,
By manipulating people for their sinister agendas and whims.
Those very people who abuse your quality and goal,
Are the same people who compromise and lose their soul.

To end on a positive, I must confess.
You are innately a good trait for connection, life and business.
You help inspire action in others that are involved.
You help inspire people to be courageous and positively evolve.

D is for Divergent Thinking

You are like a vibrant dance of the mind.
Where creativity takes the lead and multiple unique solutions to find.
It springs forth the will to tackle open-ended challenges.
Instead of chasing after a single, definitive answer.

You are a dynamic process celebrates the beauty of imagination,
As well as flexibility, and the thrill of exploring a universe of possibilities.
Imagining your brain as a canvas, splashed with spontaneous ideas, free-flowing.
This is the essence of divergent thinking, working together to unravel a problem.

Dubbed as a sort of lateral thinking, where the goal is to generate a plethora,
A plethora of innovative ideas and pathways to resolution.
At its core, you are an unrestricted journey through the landscape of thought,
Where there are no right or wrong answers to approach a situation of sorts.

You thrive on spontaneity, inviting one to explore every nook and cranny,
Of potential solutions and outcomes without the weight of judgment, uncanny.
Some telltale signs of you, divergent thinking, include the ability to build and see,
Others' ideas, envisioning the grander scheme of things, and dreaming what could be.

E is for Efficacious

You derive from the Latin word efficere, meaning "to accomplish"
Combined with the suffix -ious, which conveys a sense of fullness.
You are a term that embodies the power to achieve desired outcomes.
A hallmark of success in action.

Hinting a unique quality or virtue that bestows effective strength.
In the journey of life, you steer human destinies to create meaningful change.
And there's a deep-seated desire to see one's actions as valuable and morally sound.
You, efficacious signify the ability to bring about an intended effect and result.

E is for Empathy

You are like a magical lens that allows us to step into someone else's world.
Feeling their joys and sorrows as if they were our very own.
When we don the shoes of another, we often find ourselves compelled to act,
Act with kindness, striving to uplift their spirits and ease their burdens.

You are a beautiful state of being, that not only alleviates other's distress,
But also soothes our own hearts and traumatic tests.
For those who face early-life challenges, they develop a heightened sense of you.
Mainly as a protective mechanism, enabling to anticipate the actions of others too.

It's a fascinating link on how the more intense the trauma, the deeper you sink.
You are a remarkable skill that enriches our lives,
Fostering connections and nurturing compassion,
Engaging the world around us, to help us feel alive.

You are a precious trait and thread that weaves our social fabric.
Creating bonds that are essential for our well-being.

Feeling connected to others is vital; it's the heartbeat of human relationships,
You make us feel cherished and cared for, while immersing in shared hardships.

While your journey can be incredibly fulfilling, it can also be draining as well.
Deep connections can sometimes lead us to lose sight of ourselves.
Living like you, empathetically, means embracing the emotional struggles of people.
It's about sharing in their pain, offering prayers, and shedding tears to heal.

F is for Fervent

Tracing back to the Latin verb meaning to boil or glow,
You are hinting the heat of an emotion that grows.
You dance with passion and sincerity,
Embodying the essence of strong emotions and beliefs unwavering.

When I use you, I picture someone who champions art and culture with a fiery spirit,
Or even someone whose heart beats with intensity and admiration linked.

You are a word to describe the captivating brilliance and hope for this world.
You even paint a picture for cause, a dream, or a person.
Many people who desire visibly and invisibly to step into the spotlight,
Will have you, fervent, as their aspirations for knowledge, success, and positive vibes.

G is for Glorious

You are a treasure trove of meanings,
Each one painting a vivid picture of life's many wonders and feelings.
When it comes to feelings of joy and delight,
I often find myself calling a cherished memory in mind.

A memory that makes me feel delightful, fine, wonderful.
Such feelings make me excellently dance around the idea of what's plentiful.
Then, in the realm of achievement, you take on a new flair,
Perfect for celebrating a remarkable career, or any triumphant victory to share.

Here, it shines like something or someone illustrious or famous
You shine by wrapping one in warmth cheer and jubilation.
A breathtaking spring morning or a mesmerizing sunset,
Is what resonating with you in a splendid and resplendent context.

You, my love, embody grandeur, a brilliant masterpiece.
You stand tall and magnificent,
Celebrating the awe-inspiring nature of creativity.

H is for Hunky Dory

Everything is just peachy, satisfactory, splendid, all good.
Life is like a warm hug on a chilly day in the neighbourhood.
After landing that dream job and settling into a charming new two -story house,
I found myself living life with no hassle or self- doubt.

That's the beauty of it! Isn't it my friend?
When you can casually ask, "How's it going?" and someone responds with,
"Everything is going as planned".

Essentially when situations are all well,
I find myself feeling downright swell.
And whenever I find myself captured in a perfect moment in time.
It's all sunshine and rainbows, so sublime.

I is for Ingenious

You refer to someone who is exceptionally clever,
Showcasing creativity and a resourcefulness flair.
On the other hand, you can also describe a person who embodies honesty,
A sort of straightforwardness, and a certain innocence.

Painting a picture of individuals who possess a child-like simplicity and openness,
You spring from the word 'genius' embodied in individual actions and words.
As humans, I consider that we all possess a spark of ingenuity within us.
I've been captivated by many people who highlight this trait as inherent.

Let it be on the record and mission from now on,
That the ingenious trait is retold as a present trait in everyone.
It is not a trait reserved for renowned scientists, politicians or creatives,
Ingenious, is an innate trait not dependent on environment or life experience.

J is for Jovial

Mama, you are someone who radiates happiness and warmth,
A delightful atmosphere that lifts the spirits.
You are not just cheerful but also irresistibly charming
With a kind smile that lights up the room in any gathering.

Mama, your personality makes you instantly likable.
I can always count on you for laughter and good vibes.
In our conversations, I will always reminisce the best times,
Times when you struck me fondly and helped me fly.

A truly jovial fellow is what you are.
A jovial soul with a laid-back charm.
Your jovial spirit makes you a cheerful and animated joy to be around.
And so, I am lucky and blessed to have you, a jovial mama, all round.

K is for Karma

You're a renowned ancient Indian concept.
Apparently, you come alive after a person's actions.
"What goes around comes around", a common saying to describe how you work.
Good karma or bad karma depends on an individual's reserve.

"What you sow is what you reap", also explains how you express in life.
Clearly, all consequences from you, relate to a person's current and previous lives.
You are a relationship between a person's mental or physical state.
You are the chain of events that invokes personal fates.

You lay down the law that whatever thoughts or energy anyone puts out, will come back. Good or bad are the simple terms to differentiate what we lack,
What a person wants, is different to what they deserve.
You embody the concept of "those who are served".

Karma, you underscore how life doesn't just happen by fate.
People can be a co-creator and product of the choices they make.
Intentions are everything for you to come through,
With good intentions, you, good karma, will unceremoniously breakthrough.

L is for Lavish

You paint a picture of opulence and embody grandeur all the time,
Suggesting that something is not only elaborate but also impressively costly.
Living a life of abundance, dubs a Coldplay standard "Good life"
Transcending mere financial achievement only.

It's about striking a harmonious chord between saving and splurging.
Balancing work with personal connections,
And blending practicality with joy burning.

To "live lavishly" implies embracing a lifestyle that is both extravagant and awe-inspiring, Often fuelled by substantial financial resources aligning.
For instance, one might say that I relished my lavish lifestyle,
A privilege of affluent upbringing, and a life with God by my side.

M is for Mythical

A mindset steeped in you, whether it's a conscious choice or a subtle undercurrent, Intertwined with our understanding of the world around us.
Picture a being born from the depths of imagination—a character that dances through.
Through the pages of legends, myths, and tales spun from fiction, old and new.

Anything that carries a mythic essence draws inspiration from age-old stories or fables.
Can be considered mythical, either lesser known or famous.
I recall the myth of the legendary Loch Ness Monster,
As well as the Ancient world's plethora gods and goddesses.

Mythical, this term evokes a sense of wonder and intrigue.
Sometimes, for some individuals, it shines brighter than one can conceive.
Take the unicorn, for example—a majestic white horse adorned with a spiralling horn,
And remains beloved in tales around the globe.

So, what does mythical thinking look like?
Well, it would seem it weaves together mental and personal tides.
It can even help us make sense of our memories,
Transforming seemingly chaotic experiences into meaningful lives.

N is for Neurodivergence

Celebrate the unique ways in which some brains dance to their own rhythm
Offer a fresh perspective on how individuals experience the world's whims.
Championing the idea of acceptance and inclusion is key,
For steering clear of the outdated labels of "normal" and "abnormalities"

While the journey of brain development may follow a similar path for everyone,
The destination is anything but identical to one.
To be neurodivergent is to possess a mind that operates outside the conventional Outside the conventional norms, showcasing differences in social interactions.

Even learning styles, communication methods, and sensory perceptions vary.
And navigating the twists and turns of work or family life can be scary.
Scary in the sense of a daunting task, not a mythical beast.
Amplifying symptoms leading to meltdowns or anxiety.

Life is woven with distinct strengths and tests,
Often contrasting with neurotypical brains and their experiences.
The manifestations of neurodivergence can range from subtle to strikingly obvious,
Yet, amidst these challenges, neurodivergent individuals thrive like everyone else.

O is for Oasis

You literally refer to a lush spot amidst the barren desert.
You also serve as a metaphor for those serene havens we cherish.
Oasis, you are a fertile refuge nourished by a source of fresh water,
Standing in stark contrast to the surrounding arid landscape that can't be bought.

These green havens, which can range from a cluster of date palms,
Encircle a well to sprawling cities with flourishing farms.
Vital for travellers, an Oasis offers rest, shade, sustenance, and hydration,
And in many cultures, an Oasis is revered and recognised as a sacred space.

In our daily suburban lives, perhaps the home is the personal oasis,
A sanctuary where you can momentarily escape the hustle and bustle of life.
In another broader sense, an oasis in life represents a tranquil retreat,
A retreat that alleviates the pressures of our everyday feat.

Perhaps you have an imagined sanctuary or a delightful diversion from the mundane. For instance, you might think of an actor or singer bringing your mind calmness again.
On a spiritual level, an Oasis embodies the presence of God alone.
A place where one can experience His grace, goodness, and glorious throne.

Whatever your Oasis definition may be,
I hope it's a space for fellowship and friendship with the people you love and see.
Let the Divine fill your heart's desires like a deer who pants for water in the desert.
May your Oasis be founded in your heart, refreshing your journey in this life.

P is for Picturesque

You paint a vivid picture of something that is visually delightful or charming.

Reminiscent of a beautiful scene captured in a frame, you evoke emotions strikingly.

As graphic imagery dances in the mind's eye, you are characterised by sublime mystery,

A mystery like a quaint fishing village or the lush expanse of the Brazilian jungle.

Remember how Christopher Hussey, once famously mused,

How picturesque scenery are also characterized by what's gentle and smooth.

Thriving on roughness and unexpected distinctions,

The picturesque embraces irregular forms, colours, lighting, and even dictions.

So join me now, let's embark on a journey to some of the world's most picturesque locales,

From an enchanting island, a treasure trove of natural wonders,

Cascading waterfalls, black-sand beaches, the mesmerizing glow of the northern lights,

To the great pyramids of Egypt, the great wall of China, and the New York city life.

Travel some more my friend, get your passport stamped in more picturesque memories.

From now Hạ Long Bay, Salar De Uyuni, and Bagan, Myanmar,

To other marvels such as Iguazu Falls, and Banff National Park in Canada.

All places cannot be listed in one go, but these are examples of picturesque places to behold.

Indeed, without a shadow of doubt, picturesque is an ideal of any place.

It serves as a delightful intersection of sublime journey beauty and grace.

While beauty is often linked to define picturesque essence.

Picturesque can also be definite as appreciation of sceneries, and people present.

Q is for Quest

I am on a journey and mission to accomplish,
Goals that go beyond comfort.
From overcoming challenges and solving problems.
I fulfil my specific purpose.

Unlike in narrative media such as literature, films, video games, and role-plays,
Where the protagonist embarks on an adventure that goes on for days.
My quest will result in personal growth.
Ideally, an acquisition of knowledge and rewards.

My quest for finding purpose and meaning is certainly not new.
It's just that I haven't felt the need of articulating like I always do.
With the limited time we have in this lifetime, I find the need to express,
How each one of us, can dare to be different from the rest.

At different stages of life, we can face a time when the question becomes inevitable.
A sort of innate yearning to find the reason why we are here after all.
Usually, people like me would shy away from talking about what is uncomfortable.
But with meaning and purpose, we can empower ourselves and other people.

Starting with my workplace, a place I love to thrive in.
I learn how my reason for existence is much more than just work,
It comes from within.

With this distinction, I can understand how an individual purpose,
And an organization's purpose are two different things.
So, if I had exchanged one for the other, it's up to me to fix it.
I cannot be blaming anyone or organization, for not helping me find my purpose or live.

My quest is finding my purpose.
I am glad to finally accept it.
And although, I currently have numerous quests to complete,
I am ready to take it day by day, and live.

R is for Renew

You are like a refreshing breeze that sweeps through your life,
Invigorating both your body and spirit.
It's a journey of self-improvement that can elevate your inner fight,
A fight with the seen and unseen issues that disrupt your rhythm.

You are a path for productive, clear-headed, and joyful living.
Yet, to embark on this path, I must embrace the art of continuous growth.
This means acquiring new skills, setting ambitious goals,
It's about taking an active role in your life rather than settling.

You are also a perfect opportunity to hit the reset button.
To breathe new life into the daily routine, you help us be dignified.
In the realm of spirituality, God's spirit flows to make us signified,
And empowered to renew ourselves daily, keeping our spirits vibrant and alive.

S is for Sustainable

Embracing sustainable living is like embarking on a journey towards a brighter future.
It's all about making mindful choices that enhance the quality of life for everyone.
The essence of sustainability lies in fulfilling our current needs,
Optimizing the generations to come, and their overall well-being.

Sustainable lifestyles encompass an embroidery of habits and social stints,
As well as decisions that aim to lessen our environmental footprints.
Think lower CO_2 emissions, and minimized waste,
As well as reduced resource consumption for days.

While fostering fair socio-economic growth and a higher quality of life
Embracing sustainability is vital for safeguarding our planet, crystal tight.
People, invaluable resources next to clean air, fresh oxygen, and crystal-clear water,
Sustainable living protects diverse habitats of countless flora and fauna.

By adopting eco-friendly habits, we can reduce pollution and save energy.

We can support local businesses, choose recycle habits, and promote sustainability.

Considering the charm of purchasing items crafted from recycled materials

Many cosmetics brands now offer products in containers made from repurposed goods.

You can also discover clothing, bedding, and furniture that embody the spirit of recycling.

A practise is not just beneficial for our health, but also for the planet's wellbeing.

In the end, sustainable living fosters a harmonious connection and presence,

With our environment and others around the world, paving a more balanced existence.

T is for Thoughts

You are the idea and opinion produced by thinking.
You occur suddenly in the mind without letting an idea sink in.
You are the inner landscape of the mind, influencing reality.
You sometimes come intrusively and by surprise, questioning our humanity.

In the grand scheme of things, it is clear to me that you have been puzzling me.
For many years, if I may add, thoughts, have made me differentiate the good and bad.
I guess I hadn't addressed this realisation: that I don't always see things like others,
This makes me begin to further imagine and wonder.

I wonder what is going on inside other people's minds.
I consider what form does their stream of consciousness take,
Rhetorical questions come through, starting with:
Could my thoughts about a situation or person, be entirely different from you?

Metacognition is thinking about your thoughts, which makes it hard.
You, like me, may have heard of inner voice, an internal monologue.
Your emotions, complex, and abstract ideas mesh all together to be,
Thoughts that dictate our decisions and perceptions of reality.

You may then ask why certain things pop into the mind?
Or what makes someone prone to depression or anxiety all the time?
I am not saying that it's easy to have control over our thoughts,
But I still believe we can try to be conscious on how we feel.

Through consciousness on how we feel, maybe we can subsequently do something,
Especially during the sometimes-insidious life events that terror our entire being.
Thoughts, you are the Lego blocks on how one shapes and creates their life.
You are an avenue in times of crisis and growth, to rise like a phoenix from the ashes and thrive.

It may not be easy to break free from the autopilot that controls our minds,
Yet, the harder it may seem, there is more than meets the eye.
You will learn that transforming and shifting your thoughts for better, is doable,
And once you get the hang of it, you will become unstoppable.

T is for Thriving

To truly thrive in life is to bask in success, health, and strength.
Achieving a harmonious state of well-being across all dimensions of existence.
It transcends mere survival, embracing the journey of personal evolution.

The essence of 'thrive' is beautifully captured in the dictionary.
As 'to prosper, be fortunate or successful' gracefully.
Its essence is to grow or develop vigorously.
Thriving is like a vibrant dance of resilience and self-improvement simultaneously.

Among the strengths that resonate most profoundly is perseverance.
The unwavering spirit to push through challenges with curiosity, and kindness.
Other vibrant tips that help one flourish in their garden life.
Is to be intentional in shaping the day, weaving good habits in mind.

Thriving is about forging a connection with your authentic self.
Enhancing your self-awareness, living in harmony, and prioritising your health.
Thriving is about crafting a life where joy and positivity are the everyday norm,
Rather than mislaying yourself in uncharted territories, that often leave you torn.

U is for Utopia

First introduced by Sir Thomas More,
You paint a picture of an idyllic island society in the New World.
A concept sparking inspiration across various fields,
From architecture to social networks, and sustainable ideals.

You are a whimsical vision of a flawless society.
A dreamland where harmony reigns supreme,
And every individual is treated with the utmost respect and equality.

Picture a world where safety is a given.
Citizens thrive in a nurturing environment, freedom.
In this fantastical realm, a kind-hearted government watches over its people,
Ensuring their well-being and security is fair and equal.

Here, everyone is valued equally,
And social and moral ideals are cherished greatly.
Nature is not just a backdrop but a revered partner in the dance of life,
Embraced and protected by all in sight.

You invite us to broaden our horizons,
Encouraging us to view the world, even its flaws, with fresh eyes.
And with fresh eyes comes optimistic lens of you, utopian societies.
A utopian society that helps, you and me, envision endless possibilities.

V is for Victorious

To be you- victorious- means anger at God subsides.
You no longer blame Him and understand that He is always on time.
After all, it was the enemy of God- the devil- whose purpose was to make us blame.
To blame God and renounce Him, sends his to a Hellish highway.

The enemy of God, Satan, whose purpose is to try to get you and I to curse God's name,
As well as renounce God as we pour Him with the blame.
Just as Satan tried to tamper the patience of Job,
Our true and lasting victory is found from our faith and trust in God.

Victorious, you are a state that encourages us to trust in God's power.
Acknowledging you, victorious, results from divine intervention and reliance.
Particularly, on the love and strength provided by God, our Heavenly Father.

Quit relying on your own human strength, so fickle.
Cry out to God and repent of any unknown and known sins.
Remain accountable.

As you passionately pursue God, you will find victorious there.
Be sure to then fight the good fight,
Refuse to give up on your soul's purpose.
Then, you will find yourself victorious daily, anytime and anywhere.

W is for Wanderlust

You are a delightful German term that combines:
Wander to roam, and a lust to desire.
You encapsulate more than just a yearning for travel.
You are the insatiable urge to uncover the mysteries of the world.

It's that irresistible itch that compels me to explore uncharted territories.
To seek out the hidden gems that await my Indianna Jones' style discoveries.
It's this fervent desire to roam, a reflection of a deeper longing.
A craving to break free from the mundane and dive into the unknown coming.

Exhilarating, I find myself driven by various motivations.
From personal growth, stagnation, to escape and dissatisfaction.
Your being manifests in many ways.
Making me daydream about my next getaways.

Ultimately, the predictable nature of routine, leads to a dulling of the senses
Enter in, wanderlust, the ticket to escape the monotony of daily presence.
Wanderlust, you stimulate a life opportunity, an adventurous state.
You guide people including fearful people like me, to embrace the wonders that await!

.

X is for Xanadu

Inspired by Samuel Taylor Coleridge's enchanting portrayal in "Kubla Khan"
You have come to symbolize the follies small and extravagant.
You are also the name that dances through the ages.
Channelling images of grandeur follies and praises.

Much like the infamous Charles Foster Kane and Michael Jackson,
You have drawn mythical realm of indulgence for comparison.
You are the term that can embody a multitude of concepts.
A haven of beauty and luxury, to a breathtaking allure and sanctuary.

In the realm of botany, you are affectionately dubbed the living air filter.
Boasting a plethora of benefits that none can alter.
Spiritually, you resonate in various forms and alluring beams.
From the Philodendron Xanadu plant, a historic city in China, to the humble Joshua Tree.

Across cultures, you symbolize growth, resilience, and vitality.
Your verdant leaves serve as a reminder of life's unwavering spirit that flees.
Xanadu, you a cherished addition to any indoor oasis and state of mind,
You are like a sanctuary of literary wonder, as well as the absurdity of opulent lifestyles.

Y is for Yesteryear

You are a charming literary expression that evokes the essence of times.
A nod to the past or an era gone by.
Originally, both the French term "antan" and "yesteryear"
You are simply referred to as so "last year".

But over time, your meanings have expanded to encompass a broader sense.
A sense of nostalgia for days long past and present tense.
It can paint a picture of a tapestry woven from the threads of history.
Or even the distant epochs that lie beyond the reach of our memories.

One may even fondly reminisce about,
All "the Hollywood stars of yesteryear", who can count?
You can include delightful phrases like auld langsyne,
The good old days, old times, and cherished pastimes that amount.

Encapsulate.
Certainly, you encapsulate the collective experiences of the past.
Reaching back to times immemorial and eras that seem to drift from our grasp.

To illustrate the use of you, yesteryear, I would consider these examples:
I play music just as it was performed in yesteryear.
I revel the humble pencils and paper tablets of yesteryear, which are now replaced,
By sleek pixels and electronic tablets.

In essence, you, yesteryear, serve as a delightful snapshot and reminder,
Of the rich tapestry of our past, encompassing both the collective memory binder.
Yet, you are more than just collective memories and the distant times that linger on,
You are like a chocolate assortment of nostalgia for every tongue.

A is for Ally

You are a mode that people cannot prepare for.
You encourage people to care for other people.
You are the path to doing what is right.
You are the path that replaces darkness with light.

No one wakes up automatically to be,
A person who cares for topics that matter lately.
To be you, means to invest in this world.
Making it better, safer, and kinder as well.

You make us use our privilege to support and help marginalized communities.
You remind us that love is action, and action is needed to stop oppression.
You clothe us in courage to stand in solidarity there and here.
You motivate us to challenge the status quo, making where we stand as clear.

All in all, being you, an ally, is an ongoing work of art.
It's a delicate process that requires working from the heart.
It's also important to be humble while speaking up and standing your ground.
Being an ally, is a state of life that fosters unity that is profound.

A is for Ambiguous

You are the feeling of being uncertain from a person or situation.
You can be the answer to many possibilities and motivations.
You are something unclear with a myriad of meanings.
You are not easily resolved in language, art, or decision-making.

There are so many instances of you in life journeys.
Some synonyms of you include dark, enigmatic, cryptic, and vaguely.
Indeed, you are present in many aspects of a mundane sights.
Despite the cons, you contain numerous benefits in the daily life.

Given the numerous benefits that come from you.
It is important to address what one can learn to do.
With you, one can learn to embrace curiosities.
Asking questions that explore different interpretations and possibilities.

While many people strive and yearn to get rid of you,
There is beauty in embracing, using, and applying you.
You help one recognize the value of the unknown perspective and outcome.
You, ambiguity, enrich and innovate the lives of everyone.

B is for Barren

A desolate stretch in one's journey,
Where the landscape is devoid of vibrancy, achievement or creativity.
It encapsulates those moments when dreams remain just that—dreams,
So, you find yourself ensnared in a web of isolation, doubt, and worthless feelings.

It can feel like wandering through a vast desert of hopelessness and loneliness,
Where inspiration seems to have vanished into thin air.
But the term barren" can wear many hats!
It can describe a place that cannot nurture new life in that.

A field that refuses to yield crops,
Or a mind that feels drained of fresh ideas.
It signifies a lack of fruitful outcomes,
A void where something or someone should flourish.

C is for Conspicuous

You are an adjective meaning something that is totally obvious and unavoidable.

Obvious and unavoidable to the human sight or mind.

With this logic, someone or something can be deemed as conspicuous,

Whenever another someone notices them easily.

At work, when someone, daily, is angry and bitter,

Another person can suspect that this someone is a quitter.

Likewise, when travelling to an overseas holiday, optimising anonymity so dear.

You can suspect someone as you, conspicuous, by their lifestyle and gear.

C is for Conundrum

You are the adjective that describes an intricate or difficult problem.
You confuse, make one question on what can or cannot be done.
You are used to describe general complexities that come with life.
You leave people puzzled by difficulties that bring a great deal of strife.

A common theological conundrum rests on the existence of God who is good,
And the evil and suffering in a world, with masses of people misunderstood.
You are seen in someone who can be seen as hard to understand.
You are seen in someone who appears nice to strangers, yet not for a familial man.

You are present and active in situations, sometimes which are fickle.
From brainteasers, enigmas, to questions and riddles.
And in times, where we feel like we can't figure someone out.
We tend to call them a 'personal conundrum'— inside and out.

Regarding an existential conundrum which many including myself have to say.
You are explored through literature just the same.
Many creatives have worked to explore the matters of either nature or the heart,
Yet, many fail to realize that you, the conundrum, are like an ambiguous work of art.

D is for Dainty

You are the small, delicate, and pretty one, moving cautiously.
You describe a child, tea set or food delicacy.
Innately delicate, pretty, charming, and fine,
Are all the synonyms for you, rightly aligned.

Alas, for the women to be called you, it is considered a backward compliment.
It implies that the said women who are called you, are weaker than fellow men.
And so I must say that it is a shame to witness a shift like this:
A shift from you, dainty, becoming synonymous with feeble weakness.

D is for Disconcerting

You are that unsettling feeling that creeps in,
Leaving me anxious, confused, or even a tad embarrassed from sin.
You are the kind of sensation that can throw anyone off their game,
Making me feel a bit out of sorts, wild ambitions that need a tame.

Imagining my little brother who acts like an older brother to me,
Having wild ambitions of world domination and enslaving humanity.
I would not have fathomed, and I might chuckle at the improbability of this happening
Yet, the possibility, although minuscule, would still make me feel disconcerting.

Think now of a concert, you know the one, where everything flows harmoniously.
Now, picture anything that disrupts that rhythm—
Like a chaotic band rehearsal ending in a shouting match, unceremoniously.
Unless, of course, they're a punk band, in which case, this could be part of the show!

There's that quirky habit of bursting into laughter during interviews for a job
This is the epitome of disconcerting,
And not the best way to land a job.

Here are a few more examples of things that have left me feeling disconcerted:
From an unexpected twist that derails my carefully laid plans
To a piercing gaze or awkward silence that hangs heavy in the air.

In essence, all the disconcerting moments that you'll inevitably experience too,
Are those little jolts that remind us how unpredictable life is
And how sometimes there is nothing we can do.

E is for Evoke

Summoning forth memories, emotions, or vivid images from the depths of our minds.
A familiar scent, a nostalgic sound, or a vibrant colour you deeply like.
From your school days, illustrative sentences can whisk you back in time,
Igniting cherished recollections, a wave of nostalgia like a 'final destination' sign.

Diving into the realm of psychology, you are a fascinating principle.
For you suggest that interactions spark reactions in others, sometimes detrimental.
You and I may think that responses are unrelated to anyone of us,
But this dance of give-and-take in evoking, manifests in positive and negative sums.

E is for Equanimity

How do we discover a serene sanctuary within ourselves?
Especially when life's tempests rage around us as well?
How can we hone our ability to stay calm and centred?
Even when faced with adversity that makes us emotionally tender?

You are the art of maintaining tranquillity and balance,
Particularly amidst all of life's challenges.
Even when the trials, twists, and turns of our life reign.
You make us fully present, aware of your surroundings, yet not emotionally swept away.

The key to unlocking your door towards inner peace,
Lies in the practice of you, equanimity.
You are a psychological equilibrium that empowers us to gracefully navigate,
All the unpredictable twists and turns that life throws our way.

Equanimity, you are not just a passive state but a mindset.
You are a new skill that any fool can nurture.
Intertwined with concepts like resilience, emotional regulation, and mindfulness,
You echoed ancient Stoic philosophers and their golden nuggets of wisdom.

Even the modern Research by Gross and John (2003) reveal,
How the people who master emotional regulation, tend to exhibit greater equanimity.
So, by learning to understand and manage our emotions,
We can foster this inner calm, enhancing our equanimity during any commotion.

E is for Equilibrium

Finding harmony in life is like mastering the delicate dance,
A dance between contrasting forces—a graceful balancing act.
Between one's intellect and emotions, one must navigate valleys and peaks,
From the triumphs and setbacks to the life lessons that bring laughter and tears.

Achieving this equilibrium means carving out precious moments,
Moments for what truly resonates with your soul.
All while being flexible as your aspirations, priorities, and responsibilities evolve,
It is essential to balance and make yourself a priority to behold.

Make yourself a priority is not a selfish act.
Rather, it involves scheduling "me time" that embraces contentment at last.
To be intentional, requires a balance of supply and demand.
It is a serene, sweet spot where all the competing forces of life, find their balance.

So, what does my life's equilibrium look like?
Well for me, it's about harmonizing my inner self with the outside.
I've learned through hardships and failure,
That I must respect my own boundaries and those of others.

When life feels overwhelming, it's now perfectly fine for me to pause and wait,

Take a breath, and then gracefully take a leap of faith.
Truly, I believe every action or perspective has a higher purpose.

My life is and will forever be, an intentional energy with a vibrant pulse.

E is for Evoke

Summoning forth memories, emotions, or vivid images from the depths of our minds.
A familiar scent, a nostalgic sound, or a vibrant colour you deeply like.
From your school days, illustrative sentences can whisk you back in time,
Igniting cherished recollections, a wave of nostalgia like a 'final destination' sign.

Diving into the realm of psychology, you are a fascinating principle.
For you suggest that interactions spark reactions in others, sometimes detrimental.
You and I may think that responses are unrelated to anyone of us,
But this dance of give-and-take in evoking, manifests in positive and negative sums.

E is for Exodus

Springing from Greek roots that translates to "exit" or "departure,"
You are the monumental event believed to- around 1240 or 1440 BC- unfolded.
Tradition whispers that Moses, the legendary figure, penned the book of Exodus.
A book that chronicled the gripping saga of the Israelites who left Egyptian land.

Started from the bottom, shackled by Pharaoh's tyranny,
The Israelites were finally liberated by a divinely appointed leader—Moses.
Moses' mission was God ordained to guide the Israelites to freedom at last,
A journey that would lead to the land promised to them, known as Canaan.

Within the pages of Exodus, God is unveiled as someone deeply invested,
Invested in all of the affairs of humanity.
Let it be far from me to say what your Exodus is now.
It's a modern world for modern people, but I hope our trust in God is still sound.

Like the Israelites who were downtrodden in their Exodus , over 2000 years ago.
You and I can give our life Exodus a fair go.
He listens to prayers, responds to cries for help, and orchestrates salvation,
Even when we don't understand His own unique style and timing, we can be patient.

As the stories are true as truth can be,
This narrative of Exodus teaches us what to anticipate from God especially.
Instilling in us the courage to trust Him even in our darkest hours.
Exodus illustrates how God in this modern day and age, is tirelessly working to be ours.

He exits, He is here, and forever will be with us all.
He works to rescue the world from the grips of sin, death, and the devil.
In our lives, the "Exodus moments" signifies what makes a breakthrough,
Breakthroughs from oppressive circumstances, leading to eternal life, brand new.

F is for Flippant

You are the tossing of a playful wink into a serious conversation,
Often leaving others scratching their heads in personal reservation.
Imagine losing a hefty sum of money and someone quips,
"Better luck next time you stick!"

The essence of you, is where humour overshadows gravity.
To be you, is to dance on the edge of disrespect.
Treating weighty matters with uncalled for light-heartedness.

Picture a teenager, caught red-handed for missing curfew,
Retorting to their parent or carer with a casual "Whatever",
without further ado.
Such an offhand response, drips with sarcasm,
Irking parents or carers on their teenager's hint of rebellion.

From answering a serious inquiry with a cheeky quip,
To overlooking personal achievements and trivializing important issues quick.
In essence, you, flippant behaviour, can be understood as treating serious topics lightly.
Living almost like a carefree attitude, often to the annoyance of others rightly.

G is for Gobbledygook

It's a baffling babble that leaves you scratching your head.
A jumble of grandiloquent terms that seem to float in the ether end.
Confusion, picture a mechanic attempting to unravel the mysteries of your car.
Only for their explanation to morph into a tangled web that goes far.

Words that sound impressive but mean absolutely nothing to you.
Much like gibberish, this linguistic labyrinth is a riddle wrapped in an enigma for you. Utterly devoid of clarity for you, the listener or reader all round.
It's a whimsical experience, capturing the essence of language bogged down.

Dancing around the point, often bogged down by jargon.
It is the unnecessarily complex phrasing that makes just carbon.
Take, for another instance, a technical manual that reads like a foreign language,
Leaving the average reader in a state of bewilderment.

Springing from a rush to communicate without the care it deserves,
Peppered with technical terms and inflated language that turns.
It is simply not needed to wrap overly formal language astray.
For we live in a world where clarity reigns supreme, so let's keep gobbledygook at bay!

H is for Haywire

You are a playful, informal expression that captures the essence of chaos.
Where things spiral out of control or take a wild turn.
You are like a rollercoaster ride gone rogue—unexpected and a bit disorienting.

Many people in my life, have shared their thoughts on the legal system,
A system which for them, has taken a detour into your kind of territory.
Another example of you is in a party plan gone wrong,
Or when the traffic lights act out, leading to a line of driver confusion.

I imagine railway tracks submerged
Sending train schedules into a frenzy undeserved.
Or a show that starts off brilliantly,
But then descends halfway, turning out terribly.

I even imagine driving your trusted car, before it flunks out on the worst possible time.
Or someone may receive unsettling news,
That not only ruins their day,
But leaves them tasting the blues.

When you are in this haywire state,
I recommend you try to connect with people again.
For it is through human connection and positivity,
That you'll move on from the curveballs, regaining your life footing wonderfully.

I is for Incognito

You are all about slipping into the shadows,
Concealing one's true self from prying eyes that tell-tattles.
Picture a King, you know the One, who donned a disguise as he wanders through foreign land.
But just like a King, we can also embrace the incognito lifestyle by our own hand.

We can leave our gadgets behind, the gadgets that steal our time.
Or we can encrypt our messages and mask our features too.
We can opt for a stroll instead of a ride and tread carefully on social media,
Or we can keep a watchful eye on our privacy and security.

But let's not forget the importance of style!
I for one, loved the iconic Jadde from Bratz, who had a passion for fashion all the time.
I too believe that looking sharp is essential, no matter where you are.
For me, blending into the background feels a little bit off.

Blending in the backgrounds, I think it is important if you have a mission in mind.
It may also be key to go incognito as we only get one shot at this life.
So, let's make the shot count! and while we're here, let's shine bright,
Let's shine bright like a Rihanna's diamond, instead of fading our identities, out of sight.

I is for Incorrigible

You are someone who seems utterly resistant to change,
Withholding any chance of improvement, or correction, you stay emotionally stained.
An incorrigible bully, that is who you were,
Essentially being the person who always threw the first stone.

You are always the one to throw your weight around,
No matter the consequences, your impact is negatively profound.
While you leave me carrying a hint of hopelessness,
You often bring out a comeback with a playful twist.

Being now twenty years later, I briefly ponder on who you turned out to be,
A grown adult with a past over the-top disruption to embrace and see.
At the same token, I worry that you grew up to remain just the same,
A selfish individual showing complete disregard or care, disdain.

In essence, to be incorrigible means to be a tough nut to crack,
Undeniably, you are someone who continued down a path of mischief intact.
Though, I have hope that sometimes people can change before it is relatively too late,
I still have this feeling that you grew to be unchangeable, firmly set in your ways.

I is for Ironic

Life has a funny way of throwing us curveballs, doesn't it?
Some folks argue that the ultimate twist of fate,
Is when we finally get what we wished for,
Just when we've moved onto a better state.

It's as if God has a quirky sense of timing,
Bestowing gifts upon us when we're already in our comfort zones, cozy.
Richard J. Bernstein even famously delved into his book, Ironic Life,
Unpacking the significance of irony in our everyday lives.

Here's the kicker at the end of the day,
While you may be grappling with your own struggles,
Countless others might be looking at you, wishing they could trade places today.
It's a bittersweet truth, but don't let it weigh you down.
Everyone has their own mix of highs and lows, so the irony keeps going around.

J is for Jamboree

Jamboree, you are more than just a camp
You are a transformative adventure for young souls,
Bursting with exhilarating activities,
To thrilling challenges and cringeworthy chants.

Jamboree, you give the chance for youth to forge lifelong friendships,
You are playground for personal growth and skills across a spectrum of dimensions.
Nurturing character elements: physical, intellectual, emotional, social, and spiritual.
You converge youth to engage in joyous activities, whilst cultivating leadership skills.

Indeed, this grand gathering, a vibrant tapestry of Scouts,
As well as leaders, and dedicated Jamboree Service Team members throughout, Celebrates the very essence of the Boy Scouts around the globe,
Every four years, for a magical span of 10 summer days, these Boy Scouts unite,
Unite in friendship, adventure, and personal growth.

K is for Kaput

With roots in the German word "kaputt," which translates to "destroyed or lost."
You trace back to anything that's broken, useless, or in shambles to toss.
If I am looking to spice things up, I'll use you, a playful little word that packs a punch,
Signifying something that's broken, wrecked, or simply out of touch.

When I hear you, I picture the fridge not working, making the food go bad,
Or perhaps a person changing their reputation, but more than a tad.
I think you can really toss around this term to describe anything,
Anything that's completely obliterated or stopped functioning.

K is for Knave

You are a scoundrel, a character steeped in dishonesty and lowly intentions.
You are like someone whose moral compass is decidedly askew
A crafty trickster, if you will.

Historically you have a more innocent ring to it,
Like a young servant or a lad of modest means to live.
But fast forward to modern times, and you are a label reserved for a special people,
Who are driven by greed, knave, scheming their own pockets, and stirring up trouble.

L is for Lackadaisical

Though lackadaisical might conjure images of a flower shortage,
Its true essence lies in a lack of spirit and zest for life.
A lackadaisical individual drifts through tasks with a yawn,
Offering only a whisper of effort and enthusiasm.

To be lackadaisical is to embody a certain laziness or indifference,
Showing little passion for the task at hand.
In the world of sports, young players can't be excused for lackadaisical plays,
Much like new interns can't have a lackadaisical approach to find their footing.

May we not be lackadaisical,
A certain someone who meanders through life with a lazy air,
May we not be lackadaisical,
Showing little interest, enthusiasm or care.

L is for Laconic

John, you are someone who speaks with a minimalist flair,
Using just a handful of words to convey the thoughts in there.
Often, you give off an air of nonchalance or even aloofness.
Typically, you are a man of few words.

Appeared surprisingly at ease, shedding usual guarded demeanour,
I treasure the car rides when you speak with me a little more.
You're my brother, so I know that you embrace brevity,
I give you grace that it's bordering rudeness or indifference.

Originating from the ancient Greek region of Laconia, where the Spartans were famed, You for me, are a descent of the Spartans for your succinct speech every day.
Embodying the Spartan ethos of cutting to the chase,
Your verbosity remains sharp and understated.

In essence, remember the Spartan legacy behind the term laconic,
Especially for people like my brother John, who don it.
And, for the next time you encounter someone like John,
Be sure to expect him to use a few well-chosen words to respond.

M is for Melodramatic

Originating in 19th-century France, you took the stage by storm
Oh, what a delightful spectacle!
You are a flamboyant dance of emotions,
Where feelings are amplified to the max and every little event is pitiful.

Painted with the brush of significance.
I picture a world where even the smallest mishap can be a grand tragedy.
And every sentiment is expressed,
With the fervour of a Shakespearean actor.

Your soul lives life in technicolour.
Opinions are shouted from the rooftops in every hour.
Every situation is treated like a matter of utmost importance.
A stubbed toe? Why, that's worthy of a full-blown performance.

Complete with writhing and wailing!
While this theatrical flair can be amusing from afar,
It can also tiptoe into the realm of the absurd,
Almost like someone mourning a broken pencil or broken car.

Yet, there are those who argue that you, melodramatic, deserves a standing ovation,
These same people even suggest that you're an exuberant expression.
Take it from me, I see melodramatic as a state to embrace our deepest emotions,
Captivating audiences with rapid-fire plots, going beyond the routine motions.

Outside the realm of theatre, melodramatic has come to describe anyone.

Particularly anyone who seems to be living life on a heightened emotional scale,

Someone often perceived as overreacting to the mundane ton.

My late dad lamented on all the melodramatic souls he had ever encountered,

Claiming his stomach twisted in knots around those who thrived on drama.

He shared his own choice to navigate life with a quiet introspection,

Rather than getting caught up in flamboyant displays of people of strange intention.

My late dad's reflections sparked an intrusive thought in me:

What if the line between melodrama and a passionately lived life is grey?

What if melodrama and a life lived with fervour is elusive,

And a matter of perspective at the end of the day.

Are we all just curating our image, constantly worrying about how we're perceived?

Or are we simply allowing the essence of life to flow through us, expressing ourselves,

Without noticing how melodramatic we may truly be?

N is for Naive

You traditionally were associated with behaviour or assertions,
All that display a person's inexperience in a particular ideas or functions.
A lack of sophistication and strict adherence to ideals,
Are also signs that a naive person is real.

So, when it comes to creative business, you mightn't necessarily be bad.
In fact, you may be the quality required to help someone break out a fad.
You can propel great innovations alike.
From great branding, and great marketing, you make a good compromise.

I always take away something new.
You make me remember that life's problems are very few.
Too often I neglect the good and blessings we take.
Fixating on hard times, sadness and mistakes.

It's all invented.
I recall reading that in a great book.
A book that taught me that every problem and dilemma,
Can be changed, for better, making me feel good.

In every dead end I found in my life; I remember feeling hopeless.
Until you came along, making me face the 'unsolvable' and become fearless.
With this new mindset and reframe, I've quickly learned that life is like a game.
I can pick and choose my battles and carry naivety in a different way.

You, for me, is to take things with a grain of salt.
From people's comments, society's expectations, and even strangers' insults.
For life is precious to enlarge an issue as worse than what it is.
Indeed, life is gold, a treasure for us to nurture and cherish.

I guess inside a particular frame or point of view.
You can be the data that makes the sense of self we have, become new.
Clearly, you take away the pain, going through the motions.
You support us, like a counsellor who talks through our emotions.

Walking through my business and work like Alice in Wonderland,
You inspire me to take a stance.
Without ignoring the ugly and visible facts,
You help me, you make me take a chance.

I want to spend most of my life doing things entirely clueless.
Although, I am not a big fan of the expression "leap and the net will appear",
I want to carry you, naivety, for you make me face my fears.

N is for Nonchalant

You exude an air of tranquillity, appearing effortlessly cool and unruffled,
By the chaos of life and all its' fleeting troubles.
With a laid-back demeanour, you, John, glide through situations,
Without a hint of stress or concern, you face even the serious matters.

Your indifference is always so striking to me,
John, you are a brother to all, remaining silent unless prompted,
Masking your wise insights and feelings.

Your relaxed attitude, at times made me equate you to emotional neglect.
A struggle with one's own emotions to connect.
Fortunately, I have learned that although you resonate with the nonchalant description,
You are a strong, calm, and carefree; all of which are great qualities to make a person.

O is for Odyssey

Embark on a grand adventure,
A quest that stirs the soul and ignites the mind
Embark on a thrilling trek like journey
A vibrant thread of exploration that enlightens the mind.

Picture it as a life-long expedition,
Where every twist and turn are brimming with wonder and clarity.
Picture a wilderness of life, marked by unexpected fortunes and profound discoveries.

It's a metaphorical voyage that can take many forms,
From the literal road trip across the country—complete with car troubles—
To the transformative experience of your first year in high school or work.
Every moment from the orientation of your life story, contributes to your personal saga.

The essence of an Odyssey, is beautifully captured in Homer's timeless tale,
Where the clever Odysseus navigates the trials of the Trojan War,
Learning that even the mightiest must sometimes yield to fate.

Odysseus journey also teaches us that humility can be a powerful ally,
And that the gods, too, have their limits closer than the sky.
Irrevocably, in our own lives, may can draw inspiration from the concept of an odyssey,
And may we set sail bravely discovering the magic that lies in reclaiming the unknown.

P is for Paradigm

You are like the lens through which one views the world,
Shaping the thoughts and feelings about life and everything that matters.
You are the mental images can either lifts one up or leaves them in knackers.

Perceptions—whether sunny or stormy—are all crafted by one's own mind,
Served as detached from any reality outside.
Grandly speaking, you serve as interactions of individuals,
All of which provide a rich palette of perspectives.

I remember how you, paradigm, are not action-packed.
You are simply the term to describe the world as we perceive it!
And when we talk about paradigms of self, we're diving into how you perceive identity; Your self-image—whether you see yourself as a scholar or a dreamer—shapes reality.

Q is for Quizzically

You're a delightful adjective that captures the essence of confusion or amusement. When someone appears like you, they're often wearing a look.
"What on earth is going on here?" or "That's rather peculiar!" are statements used,
To confirm your presence, is to ponder the playful dance of questions, hidden from view.

Whether you're raising a quizzical eyebrow or casting a puzzled glance sparking intrigue,
Be sure to invite a deeper conversation that can make even a snowman's heart bleed.
And be sure to remember how this world is all about embracing confusion each day,
Learn to have a sparkling curiosity about life backstories: listen to what people say.

R is for Reminisce

Ah, the art of reminiscing!
It's like opening a treasure chest filled with the gems of our past—
life experiences, Cherished memories, and captivating stories that shape who we are.

Engaging in this delightful pastime not only brings a smile to our faces,
But also offers a myriad of benefits in so many places.
For many seniors, who may grapple with feelings of sadness or monotony,
Sharing these golden moments can spark laughter and foster a sense of autonomy.

A connection with others, all while basking in the warmth of nostalgia.
Is the art of reminiscing, it is an art more than just a memory lane stroll.

Reminiscing, it's a profound journey of reflection that allows individuals to relive,
Relive all the significant milestones and rediscover their sense of purpose within.
Reminiscing, is the bridge that links the past to the present,
Helping people like you and me, to carve out a place in this world.

R is for Retrospective

You are a term hinting at a journey back in time,
While the inviting us to gaze upon what once was, or once was mine.
You are a concept that often finds its way into my life,
During birthdays or New Year's Eve, at the stroke of midnight.

As I pass through the years that go by in a blink of an eye,
I pause to reflect on my journey and assess how closely I've passed by.
With my aspirations essentially, over my shoulder of experiences and milestones,
I am retrospective to look back, illuminating my ordained path forward.

R is for Resoundingly

You carry a powerful punch that screams insanity.
You sometimes signify something done completely or with undeniable clarity.
Picture this: voters decisively turned down the tax proposal,
Or a film remake that soared to triumphant heights.

You're an unmistakable emphasis that makes a vibrant declaration loud and clear.
The very essence is about making an impact for people to fear.
You're the kind of word that echoes through the air, leaving no room for doubt.
It's a go-to adverb for anything that's not just good.

Capturing the spirit of celebration, as in a party that's a success,
Where joy reverberates through every corner at best.
So, whether it's a yes that echoes through the room outside,
It's impossible to ignore, you, resoundingly, a word that takes staggering flight.

S is for Shrewdly

You dance around the idea of possessing a wise judgment and sharp insight,
Often leading to a favourable outcome in time.
Picture this, someone astutely foresaw the stock market's tumble,
Or a lawyer who carefully selected his cases with a clever eye, not humble.

Living means navigating life with a keen awareness of circumstances,
Making choices that tip the scales in your favour.
Someone might be labelled if they snagged a house just before prices skyrocketed,
Or skilfully maneuverer through political waters.

Even many landlords have made these types of decisions,
Like placing patio heaters outside, perhaps only now realizing the benefits.
In essence, to act shrewdly is to navigate life with a clear vision and sound judgment,
A valuable trait, often leading to advantageous outcomes.

T is for Tenacity

You are like the beaming sun, shining bright with positivity!
You're like an unstoppable magnetic force that keeps pushing.
No matter the hurdles in the path,
You're the kind of person who will go to great lengths.

Embodying a fierce determination, and an unwavering spirit.
You keep striving until you hit your targets profoundly,
Regardless of how tough the journey may be.

You are often associated with success,
Refusing to throw in the towel easily.
At the core, you are a beautiful blend of grit and bravery.

When you set sight on a goal, you're bound to achieve it.
Instead of retreating at the first sign of underachievement.
You stand firm and face challenges head-on.
Cultivating clarity and remaining headstrong.

Embracing tenacity, proved to be crucial for you, as for anyone,
Aspiring to reach their goals and thrive with love on.
By nurturing this trait, we can build resilience over many years.
Inspiring others to strengthen their characters and conquer their fears.

U is for Ubiquitous

In between the realms of countable and uncountable,
You capture the essence of being everywhere at once.
An enchanting quality of omnipresence that can be felt or imagined.
When I say something is ubiquitous, I am talking about its constant presence.

I imagine a world where someone seems to be lurking around every corner.
Sugar, for instance, is a staple in our everyday meals,
While a brand's emblem has woven itself into the fabric of our daily being.

And let's not forget about the realm of technology,
A ubiquitous computing, emerging as a magical conduit for information.
Seamlessly integrating into our lives without pulling our focus away,
Technology is a world where distractions kill time every day.

From cell phones to sugar, the colour blue to screens of all sizes,
It is set to become even more prevalent,
The concept of ubiquity,
A reminder that some things are simply inescapable with time.

U is for Uncanny

Roots in the Scots and Gaelic word,
You carry a shadowy weight when used to describe individuals.
You evoke a sense of the bizarre,
Often unsettling, leaving traced residuals.
You are the psychological dance that hints eerie similarities between people.

Equal familiarity and strangeness, stirring up feelings.
Feelings that are both disconcerting and oddly reminiscent or healing.
You also emerge from various sources, challenging the lines,
Lines that separate the known from the unknown,
The conscious from the subconscious minds.

The familiar from the bizarre.
This is what creates you a threshold,
A threshold where deep revelations and self-discovery can flourish,
Spark a conversation and behold.

The uncanny valley phenomenon illustrates how human-like figures,
Be they robots, zombies, or corpses,
Can evoke an unsettling and frightening human response.

Similarly, as Freud's idea embraced,
The uncanny sensation inspires hidden thoughts and feelings to be faced.
I guess that entails repressed beliefs and cognitive dissonance,
Are spectral representations of the incongruity:
The clash between our expectations and the realities we encounter.

U is for Unperturbed

Imagine a world where the winds whisper secrets to the creaky floorboards
But instead of feeling anxious, you simply smile, knowing it's just the house.
That's the essence of being unperturbed,
It is an oasis of calm amidst the angst and confused.

To be unperturbed is to float serenely above the waves of worry and toil,
Untouched by the storms of physical or emotional turmoil.
From someone who, faced with the daunting prospect of belting out a tune,
To someone remaining cool as a cucumber, unfazed by any terrible news.

In a nutshell, being unperturbed means embracing life's little surprises,
And having grace and poise no matter what path is for you, decided.
So, the next time you find yourself in a whirlwind of chaos, which you will,
Be sure to channel that unperturbed energy and let the world swirl around you.

U is for Urgency

You are like a swift river, flowing with purpose and determination,
Pushing us to act quickly while still maintaining the work integrity.
Embodying the essence of importance and prestige,
You demand immediate attention—like the call for aid in a famine-stricken with disease.

You are the pressing need for a timely solution to a problem, micro or macro.
Sometimes, you make us find ourselves oblivious to the urgency of a certain matter.
Yet, by cultivating your sense, we can transform both our personal and professional lives,
Sparking urgency that leads to a competitive edge to be fostered and realized.

V is for Vault

There is a plethora of interpretations for the phrase "vault in life"
Ranging from captivating museum displays,
To profound metaphors that exhibit a rich textile of life.

Imagine a vault nestled within the depths of your being,
Filled with treasures of untapped potential and value that often goes unseen.
This metaphor speaks to the hidden gems that reside within us all,
A vault that draws inspiration in one's soul.

Drawing from a passage in Peter's first epistle,
Where God's unwavering protection worked as a fortress for the faithful.
Here, God is depicted as a guardian with arms like sentinels,
A grip as secure as a lock, and hands like sturdy walls.

Apart from Peter's first epistle emphasizing that faith's more precious than gold,
Forging a sacred bond between individuals and the divine hold;
It's time to explore the concept of the "vault of heaven's time".
A term referred to the imaginary dome where celestial bodies dance across the sky.

Finally, a vault can also refer to a secure physical or digital space,
Meticulously designed to safeguard sensitive information in case.
Evoking the image of a vigorous leap,
A vault is propelled by achieving something remarkable to keep.

W is for Whimsical

Dancing on the edge of the unexpected.
Embodying those delightful whims that pop into my mind.
Living life like each day's a surprise party.
Cannot wait til the party's mine.

Imagine deciding to jet off to Europe,
At the drop of a hat—now that's the spirit of living your best life!
It's a playful, unpredictable essence,
Shunning the mundane, embracing the quirky tides.

Talk about whimsical folks or ideas.
We're diving into a world that's anything but ordinary.
These are the dreamers and the jesters.
Those who sprinkle a bit of magic into the everyday.

Fondly recalling a friend with a knack for offbeat humour,
A clear fanciful, quirky, and amusing flair.
Infusing my life with a touch of enchanting ignites,
Surrounded by vibrant souls that elevate the mind.

You're a gentle nudge to find joy in the unexpected and a reminder to lighten up.
Embracing the unusual and letting my imagination run wild.
I picture your whimsical illustrations in a storybook,
And songs that twirl with charming nooks.

Spontaneous decisions that defy logic.
A whimsical person is a delightful enigma.
Full of sudden inspirations and unpredictable antics.
I too may dash off on an impromptu adventure, inviting a little whimsy into my life!

X is for Xenial

In ancient Greece, you were a term beautifully illustrated,
On the camaraderie shared among individuals from diverse cities and states.
An embodied spirit of warmth and generosity,
Extending beyond a heartfelt welcome to newcomers and visitors amicably.

You capture what it takes to show hospitality,
Highlighting the bond between hosts and their guests beautifully.
If looking for similar expressions, I would think of hospitable and blessedness.
For Xenial, you are a word to resonate the timeless value of graciousness.

Y is for Yawn

You are an involuntary brain reflex that we try to hide.
Taking a deep breath, opening our mouth wide
You are our way to react to boredom and fatigue,
As well as when we are waking up or falling asleep.

You can also be contagious for anyone who sees,
Seeing you in others, triggers your presence, or so it seems.
Associated with brain reflexes, it is clear you make us stay alert.
You help us activate our thinking brain's reserves.

Indeed, you are the brain reflex to induce us to wake up and stop dreaming.
You stimulate our environment, channelling 'Journey' to don't stop believing.
You are tied to the fact that tiredness can trigger you, need no explanation.
Yet, I'm thankful that you, yawning, can also be a source of realization.

Z is for Zesty

Embracing the zest for life means infusing your days,
With a vibrant spirit and a contagious enthusiasm that arrays.
Embracing the zest for life transforms the mundane,
Bringing an exhilarating adventure that is unplanned for the tame.

Those who embody this zest are like a breath of fresh air,
People motivated, energetic, and ready to seize every opportunity each and everywhere.
This zestful approach is closely tied to a fulfilling life,
Enhancing both mental and physical well-being in line.

Sprinkling a little more zest into your life is delightful at best,
It requires one to dream big and chase after their goals with no rest.
While remaining open to the thrill of new experiences too,
The zest immerses one to engage and appreciate the world around you.

Zest, you are a hopeful outlook that can ignite feelings of excitement.
You share the good news to people who truly want it.
May everyone taste the tangy and invigorating flavour of zest in this life,
And embrace the vibrant activities, which can make even a broken spirit, shine bright.

Z is for Zenith

Originally hailed from the realm of astronomy,
You signify the highest point a celestial body.
Reaching in its arc across the sky.
The sun achieves you, its zenith, when it stands elevated high.

Affirmative, you are a fascinating term with roots in an Arabic expression.
Translating to "the way over one's head," and it has gracefully traversed,
Through Old Spanish, Medieval Latin, and Middle French.

Indeed, you are the word that embodies the idea of reaching the ultimate high place.
Or the most triumphant phase in a person's journey or existing fate.
When you hit the zenith, you find yourself at the apex, the pinnacle, the summit—Essentially, at the very top of your game.

Winter

A is for Abuse

Adrenal glands flood my body with stress;
As my hormone friends: adrenaline and cortisol,
Have extended their visit once again.

While the logic in my brain tries and tries, to redirect.
The blood runs far enough -away- from my fragile gut again.
My muscles in preparation for physical exertion.
Raise my heart rate, blood pressure, and respiration.
Next thing I know, my body temperature rises,
And my brown skin perspires from the insides.

People say how anger feels different for everyone.
I guess they forgot to mention how repressed anger, hurts someone.

This repressed anger feels painful to hold inside,
With no outlet or guide,
I feel like I don't want to be alive.

Where I try to repress it,
I just can't get enough,
The anger crawls like ants all over my skin.
I hold my cards to myself, so tight.
I'd trade my Joker card,
For real human touch and sympathy.

I am alone. Considered crazy, to no avail.
Anger's effects go onto my skin,
Following a churning feeling
That makes my stomach go on a whim.

While my body fails,
The soul in me, attempts to save face
But with an increased and rapid heartbeat,
Sounding like the beat of a drum,
My soul's already in the grave.

So that's it?
I will just not talk anymore.
People make mistakes,
But with a narcissist it's different.
Especially when you know,
In their head, they're the victim.
They'll never admit otherwise.
No one can say they're in the wrong.

My legs go weak.
Tense muscles as I try to run.
I feel hot like a fire.
With an urge to go to the toilet.
Sweating, especially in my bloodied palms.

A pounding head
Leaves me shaking and trembling
Dizziness if effecting my mind.
Did I fall?
Or did he push me?
Should I be grateful to be alive?

Trying to answer these questions,
Leaves me in sick misery,
My body's nervous, unable to relax.
I can't explain why I am feeling guilty,
When he controls my life.

Feeling remorseful.
Yet also resentful,
Towards seeing other holy couples,
And their holy situations.
While I recognise what true, holy love looks like,
I would usually react, all irritated.
But this time, it's different.
It's like my soul has projected.
It has.

I guess that this person, who I once loved
Has now killed me.
Leaving my body lying down,
Stagnant on the marble bathroom floor.
Eternally mutilated.

B is for Broken Heart

My life right now feels so difficult and painful.
Can't deal with.
I, a former social butterfly, now withdraws in my shell.
People call it hard to work with.

Pushed into depression, my broken heart runs a season.
A season with re-run episodes including sobbing, rage, and unreason:
From finding myself not eating or sleeping for days,
To neglecting my personal hygiene as a display.

People describe brokenness as a dull ache,
While for me it is a piercing, albeit crushing sensation,
That stabs me harshly, in every way.
This pain sometimes lasts for a few seconds and then subside,
But at times it feels like its' chronic,
Hanging randomly in waves, over odd days,
And depleting me, every time.

It's like I know I am sad and disappointed,
But could care less about doing anything about it.
I'd rather live with the pain like some back pain or a migraine.
An emptiness so profound.

Over time, I find myself doubt and question:
About all my relationships, my past and present.
My mind then begins to flood with intrusive thoughts.
Making me desperate, lonely and distraught.

Reminiscing this life at night, when I try to sleep.
I imagine scenarios in my head,
Of what my life could have been.
In short, I can't help feeling complete defeat.

Over the next three days, I am always feeling like I want to go home.
No matter where I am,
Or my interesting activities planned.
I can't help feeling alone and vulnerable.

Both emotional and physical,
My heart feels like there's an open wound.
An open wound that I cannot heal or fill.

It's now six months on, and I feel like it's a lifetime,
As I experience my brain and emotions taking a deep dive.
It's the worst feeling.
Something I would not wish on my enemies.

With a broken heart often, I find myself in episodes of sobbing,
Followed by rage, and despair.
I can't eat.
I can't sleep.
I ust go deep,
Dwelling in a bottomless grief.

By grieving someone, who is still alive, and happy.
Leaves me to pick up the pieces.
Try to start again.
Live life like nothing has happened.

Now, a whole year has passed, and I feel like my survival depends,
On reuniting with what took all my willpower, ambition, and strength.

Where is my self-respect?
Where is my self-control?
I ended things and requested the person to not reach out.
But now, as I am alone at home,
I fantasize them reaching out.

I wish someone told me that breaking a relationship,
Are the hardest things you will ever do.
It's like a squeezing in your throat and chest.
A knot in your stomach that is near impossible, to fully remove.

What now matters, is that I know that being deeply sorrowful or distressed,
Will only be a season in my life.
Temporary.
Before a new season starts healing season,
Transforming my heart at best.

C is for Convoluted

This life is twisted, tortured, turbulent to a common man.
This life is complicated than what needs to be, and a chore to understand.
To reason with you is to reason excessively, nothing less of complex.
I see a complicated structure, a story that gives inferior reflex.

Having many overlapping natures and intricate stories to unfold.
This life is like a form of expression, difficultly determining how to be told.
Before deciding whether I am ready to go in or out,
Convoluted, I determine the excessively complex points, in and out.

C is for Cunning

You deceive and manipulate.
As the goal is to get what you want.
So, you'll do whatever it takes.

I found you in several individuals,
In all aspects of my life on Earth.
I see you at work, in social circles, and families as well.

Dealing with people like you can be challenging,
A person like you, always appears lovely and charming.
But undercover like a spy, are manipulative, insincere, and prideful
Always working from personal interests that are usually spiteful.

By frequently contradicting themselves, while disregarding needs of others.
People like you are very skilled at exploiting the weaknesses of others.
To make matters worse, people like you, will draw others in their games,
Provoking others emotionally, and making them feel insane.

So, what now?
What can you and I do?
Well by spotting your toxic traits- early on,
I can try to take necessary precautions and remain calm.

*To limit and diffuse your subtle command,
I'll just respond in a measured manner,
Taking the upper hand.*

*Breathe deeply.
Think carefully, I tell myself on what I want to say,
Think carefully, I plan to respond in a measured way.*

*Be assertive
I will stand up for myself.
Hold your ground firmly,
I will stand up against your hell.*

*Be clear.
I will clarify what I want and communicate it firmly.
Set boundaries.
I will express and say no when necessary.*

*Avoid being gullible.
You are the masters at making intentions look benign.
So, I'll avoid being gullible.
Falling for your kaka, all the time.*

*Protect your interests.
When dealing with you, it will be important to remember this:
For you are only ever concerned with a manipulation,
And ulterior objectives.*

Look out for yourself.
I will remember my interests and wellbeing.
Ensure that you are not vulnerable.
I will break the chains of your endless schemes.

And so, when push to comes to shove, dealing with you is problematic.
And so, it's essential to remain pragmatic.
I am ready to recognize your traits from a mile.
I am ready to get away from you, leaving gratified.

D is for Deception

You are the act—big or small, cruel or kind.
Encouraging people to believe information, that is falsified.
Lying is a common form of you, no confession.
People like you state something untrue for their protection.

Your actions usually cause one to unknowingly accept,
Something true, honest, or valid,
Even things that are left unsaid.

The act of all your works, deserve an Oscar globe and ovation.
Your fear of punishment, and your fragile ego, also drive infatuation.
I hold onto hope that people fall to avoid negative consequences,
But in your case, you lie to keep up appearances.

You're only human, an excuse I have heard and given out.
But does it make me an alien, if I don't accept that reason now?
White lies.
Like a tone could somehow pass for deceit.
What's in a tone, to absolve the lies you speak?

Perhaps, you want to ensure one doesn't fall in an unpleasant mood.
Yet, while you lie by default or omission, I can easily see it through.
What is more, there's the everyday lies that I tell myself.
"You don't mean to", "It's not your fault", and the "You just need help".

Older, but not always wiser, yet I have learned ingrained societal lies.
Lies that root from our governments from the inside.
It's like global society, at various levels: personal, family, job, and beyond.
Are held together by a massive web of deception.

D is for Dreich

Ah, the word "dreich" – a delightful little gem from the Scottish lexicon.
Capturing the essence of dreariness and gloom.
It paints a picture of days that feel heavy with sadness,
As well as dullness, and a touch of misery with madness.

With roots in Germanic language and a nod to the Old Norse "drjúgr,"
It evokes a sense of endurance and long-suffering,
Much like those endless, dreary days that seem to stretch on forever.

Imagine a day where the sun has taken a backseat,
Replaced by a dreich drizzle that sends everyone scrambling
Scrambling for their umbrellas and weatherproof jackets in lieu,
Of a day soaking up the sun, and enjoying the ocean view.

Picture a church service that feels as heavy as the clouds above,
Or a Friday morning that drags on in a monotonous haze, so long.
Even the task of tendering your beloved garden which you love to do,
Can feel dreich when the cold wind bites at your clothes and shoes.

In the realm of Scottish politics, the outlook can seem equally drear and dreich,
Especially if we let life's moments slip away.
So, whether it's the weather or the weight of the world on our shoulders,
Dreich describes those moments that come like a dead end boulder.

E is for Envy

I am feeling a mix of admiration and resentment.
It's like I appreciate another person's talents, but I harbour contempt.
Whenever I notice people's possessions
I can't help but wish I had them, and for myself, covet.

As a thorn around a rose about to bloom,
I feel choked by envy, impeding my self-inflicted gloom.
As the saying goes, envy is poison for the door of your fate.
Envy makes you feel terrible, lacking personally, and a heart brimmed with hate.

Projecting my own perceived shortcomings will be the first stop.
To help me stop comparing myself with others, non-stop.
Society's social media has buzzed me unattainable goals and high standards,
Making me feel inferior, a second-rate person, susceptible to jealousy.

As I think and write again, I try not to hate, or wish ill will.
Matter of fact, I would love to meet the people I envy in this world.
For I bet if I met them, I could soon learn and realize,
That their success, does not take away from my beautiful life.

Yes, I will try to empathize, not criticise, whenever I feel these pangs of envy.

I will, rather than covet something or someone, resort to counting my blessings.

I'll even put myself in another's person's glorious situation.

As hard as it can be, I can be rest assured that life's good, for me, as well.

F is for Fear

A state no one wants to embrace.
The background music to my everchanging life.
But by understanding why you exist.
Can help me become less vulnerable, or so I think.

Confronting you can be a daunting task at times.
Especially as it forces me to acknowledge what'll make me want to die.
Whether that's petting a wild animal, facing terminal illness, losing a loved one, or contemplating mortality,
Facing you is enough to trigger a response, both physical and emotionally.

Figuring out why I want to embrace you in my life, can truly help,
Make the 'out of comfort zone' process, easier to manage, and to manage it well.

I want to become a braver person, not only for me,
But for my future husband and future kids.
Yes, I want to become a woman of courage, kindness and commitment.

With this huge purpose in mind, I know I can be successful.
So, I will switch it up, test new paths and remain humble.
And as I switch things up, I will try everything, uncomfortable and unconventional.
I will make you: fear, loosen your grip over me, intentional.

Facing you, will be a lifelong mission and task.
There will be times when I will feel I cannot last.
Yet, I know I can muster up the strength to be brave,
For life is too short to let you: fear, take my joy away.

F is for Fragility

Life dances on a delicate tightrope, reminding us of its inherent fragility.
Each of us encounters moments that test our resilience and humanity.
From losing a cherished friend, battling illness,
To grappling with foolish choices that haunt us.

In its essence, you are the state of being easily shattered.
Often, you creep into our minds when we face hurdles that leave us scattered.
Even in creative pursuits, whispering doubts about our talents,
Your existence teachers us how life is an unpredictable wild card.

Unpredictable and full of surprises, both delightful and devastating.
You are a gentle nudge to cherish the fleeting moments taking.
Especially when loss casts a shadow over our hearts,
Contemplating our own mortality, and suffering from our past.

Recognizing you, life's fragility, can inspire a more tender intent.
Particularly in our journey on this planet, fleeting moment.
Life's fragility is a call to action to embrace what we love most,
Treasuring the beauty of today, instead of chasing tomorrow.

G is for Gaslighted

You are a colloquialism.
Loosely defined as making someone question.
The term derives from the title of the 1944 Hitchcock film 'Gaslight'.
A film where a manipulative husband,
Tries making his wife think she is losing her mind.

You are subtle, type of emotional abuse.
You make me question my perception and reality.
Ultimately, at your worst, you make me fall in a bout of insanity.

Gaslighting. You tend to sound like as follows:
"Oh, you're so dramatic"
"Oh, you're too sensitive"
"Oh, you're too emotional"
"Oh, you're imagining things, how pathetic?"

Or if you want to really spice things up.
You tend to say statements below, quite rough:
"You know you sound insane right nowt?"
"You're always making stuff up, you cow!"
"Why are making a big deal out of nothing?"
""You're acting crazy. Stop. It's all or nothing ".

You mostly show up in dating and married relationships.
But in some occasions, in friendships and family, you make an appearance. .
You are an effective technique that makes me question,
My entire reality and solid perception.

After an interaction, I walk away wondering what is wrong with me.
And in extreme cases, begin to question my own sanity.

My job is not to be the psychologist for you.
My job is to protect and care of myself, before you.
In essence, you sit under the umbrella of coercive control.
You are a covert type of emotional abuse in which the abused takes the fall.

H is for Hate

You are the noun for an 'intense dislike'.
You are the feeling felt in people's lives.
The feelings from your roots, are normal sporadically,
It only gets concerning if your feelings occur constantly.

Your kind of feelings harboured in one's heart,
Can lead to devastating effects that like a wolf to its prey, tears apart.
Feelings of rage leading to hatred, all built over a time,
Can make one vulnerable to be misaligned.

By misaligned I mean the body, mind and soul,
With you seeping through, one's organs and natural processes work poor.
Even though, I am not a doctor or scientist to give credit for,
I know that you are the form of neurosis that is harmful.

Continuing you breeds the conflict that world leaders cannot endure,
Resorting to wars that occur on a global and civil scale.
You are the bodily disease without a pharma cure,
When left continued and unnoticed, you, hatred leave one's bias unchecked.

You are the verb for bias left unchecked.
Bias being a preference either for or against.
With bias left unchecked on an individual or group,
We become affected to judge fairly through.

When you become normalized or accepted, it may even escalate into violence.
As a result, this manifestation breeds more ignorance, anger and dismay.
It attaches you to the thing or person you hate.
You are the intense repulsion that creates a mirror effect in that way.

You are the bitter-sweet paradoxical pain,
You inflate one's ego, but at the same time, can make someone repulsed by them.
Interestingly, the way to conquer you, is not love,
But a mental and emotional detachment for something or someone.

I is for Irrational

You are an adjective meaning 'not logical or reasonable'.
To be an irrational human, means to not based on good judgment.
You make people behave with swords, fists, and knives in their mouth.
You escalate the situation, whatever the size, from North to South.

To regulate a human who behaves with your qualities,
You'd need to calm down yourself and model uniformity.
Yet, I wouldn't say to someone: "You need to calm down",
For that's equivalent to telling someone who cannot swim to "just not drown".

Viewing anyone as you, means they've already succeeded,
Succeeded in riling you up and taking something too personally.
With manipulation, a part of your middle emotional brain- amygdala- is hijacked.
Leaving you blocking your rational brain and thinking everything's bad.

You make me make me intentionally act out in a way to be more upset.
In some way, the thoughts make me upset that I am becoming upset, nonsense.
Alternatively, when I replace the irrational for rational, I become serene,
Taking the emotions out of the equation, focusing on what's reality.

Ever hears the old-time saying: "When you're a hammer,
everything will look like a nail."
Well, when exuding you, the whole world looks dull and grim.
Having been on the other side, naïve, powerless, and vulnerable.
I now protect myself, taking on the journey to heal my inner child.

I have also learned that it's not irrational to promise oneself as
an adult,
That irrational people and situations faced are finished,
I can change my 'now', instead of dwelling on what's already
happened.

J is for Jealousy

You are an ugly feeling of wanting something that someone else has.
You're a disguise of fear that someone or something will take what you have.
Whenever people talk about you, people deny harbouring your feeling,
In hopes that you will sooner than later, be a feeling fleeting.

When I thought about you, I often connected it beyond relationships and love.
For me, you make a far broader impact on different areas, below and above,
Affecting mental health, fast forwarding insecurity,
You never come short of fostering my low self-esteem.

You have powerful ways to control the mind.
You sometimes lead me to take action that leads to a seemingly fulfilling life.
Being a complex emotion, you can bring the worst out of me, or really anyone.
You can make one forget all the goodness and accomplishments already done.

When you come to visit my mind, I'll be sure you don't overstay.
I will gladly open the door and lead all your baggage away.
With you gone, my life will be so much lively and better,
I will communicate to myself and live a content life serving others.

*You can watch me grow and clarify my feelings, worries,
or concerns.
You'll see that there is power in addressing any potential issues that
unknowingly hurt.
And before life becomes all too overwhelming, as it can be.
I'll shift gears and see you for who you truly are- insecurity.*

K is for Kerfuffle

You are the minor disturbance, a kind of fuss trivial to the naked eye.
You are the commotion, typically caused by a conflict inside.
By inner conflict, I mean a person who is small.
Small minded to make a situation overblown.

You retract attention, far more than what you deserve.
Overrated, overrated, overrated, I say it three times to settle how you're absurd.
Throwing into disorder, unflattering scenes, and awkwardness.
You, kerfuffle, are like a sound of a delicate object hitting a hard surface.

L is for Lust

You are an intense desire or craving for something.
You come in topics of money, power, food, smell, and sexuality,
You can be a feeling of having a strong sexual desire for another person.
You're the initial driving force that attracts us to a potential partner to keep.

You effortlessly alter the neuron chemicals in our brains.
You renew a sort of enthusiasm, sometimes making us carried away.
While this is the case, you, lust is still coined as a deadly sin,
Particularly from all the Christian theologies.

As a deadly <u>sin</u>, you, lust, are believed to spur other sins.
From immoral behaviour, adultery, to going off on a grave whim.
Adversely, you can be a powerful feeling alongside attraction and attachment.
You can make us express sexual desire for a preferred someone or partner.

You and love, work diversely and in a real way.
You and love happen differently every day.
By recognising that you, make one lose sight of realities,
It is important to pluck out the degraded eyes of you, to be psychologically free.

M is for Mistakes

Nobody is perfect, and that is okay.
We can meet someone who is wrong for us and still not breakaway
Society's timeline forces us to ignore our intuitions, until it is far too late.
Leaving us wishing there was a time machine, to prevent us from making mistakes.

You are always in our short life, coming in all shapes and sizes.
You come larger than others, some planned, and sometimes as unwelcomed surprises.
You manifest in topics related to careers, marriage, a quick divorce, or friendship breakdown.
You aim to make us give up and believe that this life is upside down.

Personally, my mistakes are in not saying 'no' when I need to.
Or giving people chances in the guise of resilience without further ado.
In every mistake and fall, my family, nuclear and extended, helped me through it all.
With the gift of family, I was understood, accepted, and never felt small.

With love and kindness, learning from you, my mistakes, became easy as breathing in and out.
My family, even friends who felt like family, helped me realise that my mistakes don't bring me down.
I had a way out.

So that is why I am glad and grateful to choose family, after God, above all else.

My family and faith are what gives me, a human who makes mistakes, blessings.

My cup is overflowing like water running from Jacob's Well.

N is for Nasty

By your definition and meaning, you are dirty and foul.
You are the term to describe something morally disgusting that makes one cowl.
You are in a disagreeable sense, something quite awful, dirty and downright unpleasant.

In a simple form, you are the opposite for any word synonymous to nice.
Your main meaning is for things or people anyone can despise.
If someone threw up or bled out in front of me, I would most definitely use your word.

You make me ignore my own values and things that matter to me.
You go against my inner core and pollute my 'secret garden' of being.
Unsurprisingly, you come to make me downtrodden and full of doubt,
You push people in my life, to never take a chance or go out.

Sometimes, you are used on the strangers who don't deserve it.
You wrap yourself in a guise of perfume when you're truly a rotten stench.
I hope that I never have to use you for an upcoming situation or event.
Yes, may you be seldom used, to describe what is inevitably unpleasant.

O is for Oppression

You are the noun meaning prolonged cruelty.
Manifesting in the treatment or exercise of any authority.
You are assigned to a multitude of identities.
Deemed 'normal' to a dominant person, who limits opportunities.

Anyone can come from a non-dominant group and experience oppression.
This refers to the combination of prejudice from people or institutions.
You create a cunning system that severely discriminates,
Against some groups of people who are unlikely to retaliate.

You help us to identify an iniquity or inequity.
Driving people to call for attention to the historical and systemic community.
From sexism, heterosexism, ableism, classism, to ageism and anti-Semitism,
You reinforce marginalized social groups, backward favouritism.

You are the seed from the tree of worldly suffering and abuse,
Subtly diminishing the life experience and divide communities through.
Mercilessly, you lead people to feel heavily burdened, a new hell.
You take the crown for stealing mental, physical, and spiritual health.

P is for Pain

You make my body's nervous system think not so well.
Every time you come into my life; you bring me a new hell.
I feel you creep up like a cockroach that makes me fall in fright,
You are a part of your body, making it think it's injured or in danger of getting tied.

You are not just a normal sensory signal.
You always like to notify in advance.
Like a teacher who puts me to the exam,
I have accumulated life experiences that are miserable.

As much as we want to be with people, we must lose people every day.
Death is something we also cannot predict or relate,
Death is as natural as the sun rising daily,
Pain, you like death, come with such intensity,

You also come to visit when a breakup occurs.
The term 'oOuch' undersells the feeling of the hurt.
Wreaking havoc for us all, you are always someone who makes us believe,
That the breakup will mark a sort of loss of romance and harmony.

You even suggest that we will somehow end up with who broke our heart.
A sort of cheeky mantra that is nonsensical logic from the start.
While this is the case, you also help us to find love we deserve to have,
Teaching us that when we're able and ready, the right one will come to us at last.

Following this life event, you come along for the ride,
Whenever a significant failure is on the tide.
You know it can be so frustrating when we work so hard on something,
To then not get the desired results that we expected as coming.

Whether it's a wasted opportunity, a competition lost, or a business bankrupt,
You, pain, remind us to do better, you like a willing and able parent, are here to teach us.
Knowing that there's room for improvement, you inspire us to continue,
Journeying towards our best in everything we decide to do.

You also remind us to not stop when we think there is nothing more to lose.
Resilience helps to embrace you, thereby taking lessons learned.
Such as life situations, or someone like a thief in the night, unheard.

You also come out from betrayal, but not like anything one could predict.
You make us trust that this must happen based on instinct.
For us to learn significant life lessons on discernment
Truly, betrayals teach us to become more mindful about the relationships we retain,
As well as the people we allow to be in our space.
You come again when people, situations or things are outgrown.
And it takes a lot of maturity, to embrace you in the unknown.
So, although there will be certain relationships that reach an expiry date.
This heart-breaking occurrence will open new experiences and fate.

Q is for Quixotic

You are a foolishly impractical, especially in the pursuit of ideals.
You are marked by rash lofty romantic or extravagantly chivalrous ideals.
Indeed, extremely idealistic, unrealistic, and impractical.
You make anyone obsessed with an impossible hope.

While all these words: fantastic, imaginary, and visionary, meaning something unreal.
You imply a devotion to romantic or chivalrous ideals.
You are unrestrained by ordinary prudence and common sense.
You are a whimsical decision made, without second thoughts of a consequence.

When someone says they are you, it is not a direct compliment as thought.
Rather, it is a suggestion that the person is living on an afterthought.
Typically, to be you, is to be overly Imaginative and out of touch.
To be you, quixotic, is to risk it all in overwhelming odds.

R is for Rudeness

You are the noun to mean a lack of manners.
Alternatively, you are the demonstration of courtesy thrown out of the spanner.
I am sure people have justified their reasons to demonstrate you.
From having a familial loss, financial issue, or simply feeling the blues.

Sometimes, you come over by surprise.
You even prompt people to be like this, without even realized.
In a hurry, time is money, people don't even reflect.
Thinking their actions are always with good intent.

You are not clear unless someone dares to ask or speak up.
It only takes someone to address another's rudeness to be seen.
You always bring on a ripple of negative impact,
You take a toll, making people's mental health far from intact.

You even sometimes pretend to be an aura of self-confidence, when you really ain't.
I don't remember self-confidence as putting people down, or even throwing shade.
At worse times, you lead withdrawal from God's work, hindering cognitive abilities.
Undoubtedly, you like to work overtime, compromising people's sensibilities.

I hope one day you will learn how you always put people in different jeopardies.
You increase stress, alter decision-making, and increase overall irritabilities.
Rudeness, you are the undermining for functioning of human beings.
So, I hope you're no longer able to play into people's vulnerabilities.

S is for Sadness

You are a difficult emotion to deal with,
Let alone and talk about with people.
Even though you are one of most natural and common human emotions,
I am not all that keen to succumb to any of it.

For me, you are like a bird above my broken heart nest.
I feel you viscerally, like a heavy gym weight, creating a heavy pressure at best.
Positively, I would frame you as a chance to reflect, or perhaps see the bright side,
But it's hard to frame you, when your creeping eats me from the inside.

Now as I grow old, I have learned that you are a natural feeling for loss,
Whether that be for a friend, family, animal, or job.
So, when you come to visit my body, I will let you be, until it's time to move on.
I will use you as a guide to keep me safe and at home.

You already have, and continue to help me reach out,
Accepting people's help,
You transform my sad moments with hilarity
And a whole lot of spiritual wealth.

T is for Toxic

Most people are very quick to label you onto others.
Yet, without taking a long, hard look at one's own behaviours,
It can be clear as the sun.
How your being can seep into anyone.

You are the poison that humans like to share,
You embody various behaviour and traits no one wants to bare.
It's easy to assign you onto others we don't like or care.
It's easy to blame your presence, to condemn people anywhere.

You may be the most present in myself, but in a private room.
I think you bring on the double standards that bring doom.
To judge another is easier with the privilege and eyes that one is without sin,
When you are the hidden and insidious sin within.

Why and why, do I behave in such a damaging and reprehensible manner?
I bet Bob the Builder never threw down an ever-toxic hammer.
The only time I want to look down at someone, anyone for that matter,
Is to bring them up and help them feel better.

Certainly, one's life principles may be fleeting, changing at any given moment of time.
But I sure as heaven, hope that I would not use you as a compromise.
So, if I act sweetly as a front, to only to make rude comments in the background,
That makes me a cesspit in the ground.

Toxic, maybe Britney Spears was onto something real, slick.
For you expand from any Hollywood-styled romantic relationship.
You are a person, including oneself, that should be prohibited.
I sure as heaven, hope that your behaviours, shan't be unwittingly exhibited.

U is for Ugly

You are a term used by bullies worldwide.
You are a word to challenge the self-esteem of victims in every side.
For you to succeed, people must accept that what people say as true.
Inadvertently collaborating to the bullying process too.

You are a term that can determine how we see ourselves.
The only opinion that matters is based on our common sense.
You do not depend on those who praise you to measure your self-worth.
You are a word that makes people loathe and hate themselves.

Even people who look different from many others all around,
You are a term that is no better or worse to resound.
And no matter what someone was taught as a young child,
When the word is used, the self-esteem subsides.

From lighter or darker skin, bigger or smaller noses,
To prominent or non-prominent ears, freckles or none, curly hair or straight woes.
None of these differences have importance in determining a person's worth,
Or whether they are subjectively ugly, should not be loved.

There are many other answers offering unsolicited advice,
You have no idea on how I have been bullied many times.
Throughout primary and my high school years, you have stuck with me like a parasite.
When someone called me ugly, they would put my self-esteem in demise.

You are the boomerang insult that reveals who are ugly from their core.
So, let's not give the people attention that they desperately cry for.
It took me time to realize that I was suffering from a being so insecure.
Feeling that the term meant I was not good enough like before.

From feeling good enough, not being pretty enough,
To being brought down too many times without a bluff.
I had an extreme habit of looking in the mirror,
Wondering if what they said was true and piling on the makeup.

It was so bad to try and cover my natural state,
Before I knew it, it became out of control, leading me to stay home for days.
At home, I would get into fights with my parents and brother,
Who kept saying I was not what the bullies had detailed to each other.

Fast forward to my early twenties, a golden age.
I have learned to not care about looking different to people's beauty gains.
For the people who called me ugly, were really the ugly ones.
Likewise, the people who now call you ugly, should never overcome.

So, if anyone is heartless and claims you are ugly too.
Be sure to screw them, and deliberately not take it to heart as true.
For insulting someone's appearance, calls for some personal introspection.
Therefore, be sure to leave it at that, ignoring people's invalidated perception.

V is for Vicious

You are the adjective for someone or something's actions,
Actions that are deliberately cruel, nasty, harmful, or violent.
Someone who is coined as you, are evil without a shadow of doubt,
You are in people or things that carry out evil intent.

A vicious blow is indeed violent and cruel.
You appear in rare cases of poisoning water, or animal abuse.
A vicious blow is an attack to the future youth,
You can be a remark so pointed and so very cruel.

People should be above the animal race,
But sometimes, people behave far worse to save face.
For instance, a vicious animal with its' habits to attack,
Can sometimes be far better than people with a weak back.

By weak backs, I mean people with no integrity.
People who act as if people are objects, and thereby shower misery.
To be vicious is to bring out a fierce disposition.
Equivalent to taking people's hearts to prison.

You do harmful things to people's unity and peace.
From creating conflict and wars, you damage everything.
You consist of a paradoxical desire and goal,
One to gain the whole world by force, while losing eternity's soul.

W is for Wicked

You are the adjective meaning evil or morally wrong.
Perhaps to describe something or someone.
To be you, is to be morally bad to all,
Someone who is ruthless, dishonest, or deliberately takes the fall.

You are something that can be slightly bad but in an attractive way.
For example, a person's sense of humour could be wicked, if enjoyable.
Yet, the most obvious way you come is through various forms of deviance
You manifest in people who cheat, steal, rape, murder, tainted innocence.

Bad things tend to happen wherever you are present and strong,
Bad things tend to happen when you are used by a certain someone.
This certain someone tends to get away with a lot,
Leaving their malfeasance being unnoticed so they never stop.

To have you, means to risk having a criminal record.
As well as constant run-ins with the police, and other authority figures.
You make people lie incessantly as if they are breathing in and out.
You make people expert in making themselves appear devout.

Truth is your nemesis in this tragic journey we call life.
Your darkness will be overcome by the truth's light.
For you, wickedness, are one of the many vanities.
You are the essence of what ruins moralities.

X is for Xebec

You were my reminder to slow down and appreciate nature's wonders.
You taught me to be resilient through challenges.
A breath of life, a primary source of momentum and confidence.
A breath of life, providing a spiritual resemblance.

I remember sailing with you all around the world.
Across the seven seas.
From islands like Fiji, Australia, and Tahiti.
I remember sailing with you in my soul effortlessly.

An essence, you helped me develop new strategies.
The breath of life.
You were the test diagnosing my communication, personal and professional,
As well as my journey navigating a spiritual life.

Being with you, embracing your light that shines,
Improved my cardiovascular health, but now with you gone, a heartbreak resides.
Whenever I see the Xebecs across the Alexandria shore,
I remember how you brought my life meaning, a meaning so pure.

Y is for Yesteryear

A time in the past,
Especially the recent past.
A way of life or set of values that no longer exists.

A town.
A very little town,
Which had little room for love,
Is now a bigger town for everyone.

My home.
A dainty home,
Which was a harbour of memories, good, bad, and ugly.
Is now sold to a lad, who acts suspiciously.

Eternal life.
Eternal life has come.
I remember my life as a blip.
The temporary deviation from God's plans.

Z is for Zestless

You are an adjective to mean a lack of interest.
Or a lack of a general will to live well.
To be you, is to have a lack of flavour.
To be bland, boring, and deflated.

With people living their best lives all around,
You make one feel a distaste for life, so profound.
From just passing or wading the days that turn into years,
You bring an existence that has little to no meaning.

From little to no meaning, comes little excitement for events or people.
You demoralize the flow and work of society, painting it all as unfruitful.
Deep down, you make one consider the grass being greener somewhere.
You, zestless, make vulnerable people spiral into despair.

www.ingramcontent.com/pod-product-compliance
Lightning Source LLC
Chambersburg PA
CBHW061147170426
43209CB00011B/1579